Hattin 1187

Saladin's greatest victory

Campaign • 19

Hattin 1187

Saladin's greatest victory

David Nicolle

Series Editor Lee Johnson

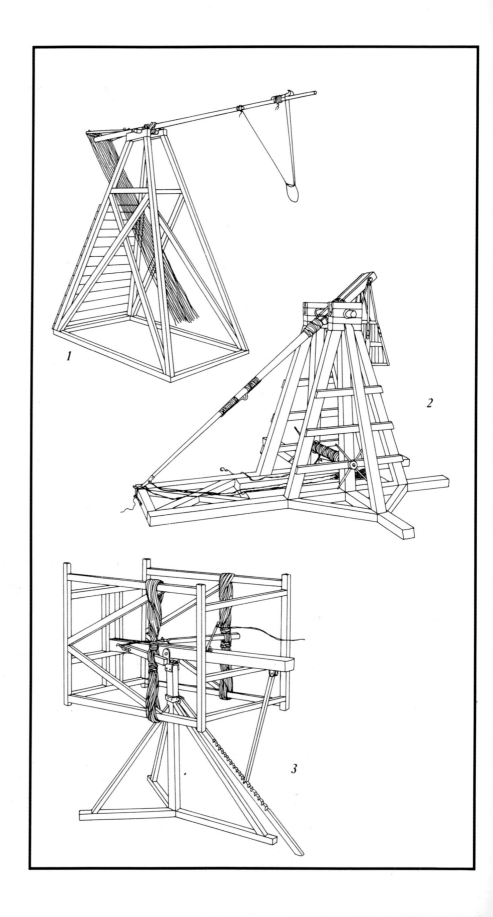

1

2

3

CONTENTS

First published in 1993 by
Osprey Publishing,
Midland House, West Way, Botley,
Oxford OX2 0PH, UK
443 Park Avenue South, New York,
NY 10016, USA
Email: info@ospreypublishing.com

CIP Data for this publication is
available from the British Library

ISBN-13: 978-1-85532-284-4

Produced by DAG Publications
Ltd for Osprey Publishing Ltd.
Colour bird's eye view illustra-
tions by Cilla Eurich.
Cartography by Micromap.
Originated by DAG
Publications in QuarkXPress via
TBL, Warley. Mono camera-
work by M&E Reproductions,
North Fambridge, Essex.

Printed in China through World
Print Ltd.

08 09 10 11 12 17 16 15 14 13 12 11 10

FOR A CATALOGUE OF ALL BOOKS
PUBLISHED BY OSPREY MILITARY
AND AVIATION PLEASE CONTACT:

NORTH AMERICA
Osprey Direct, C/o Random
House Distribution Center, 400
Hahn Road, Westminster, MD
21157, USA
E-mail: info@ospreydirect.com

ALL OTHER REGIONS
Osprey Direct, The Book Service Ltd, Distribution
Centre, Colchester Road, Frating Green, Colchester,
Essex, CO7 7DW
E-mail: customerservice@ospreypublishing.com

www.ospreypublishing.com

The Latin States in 1187

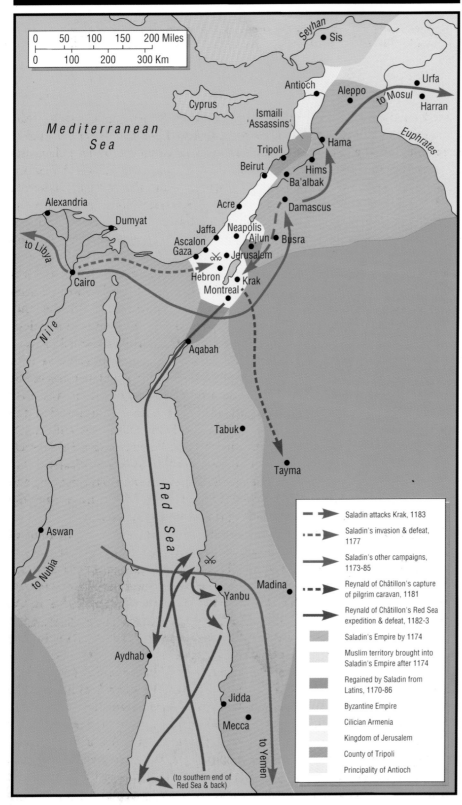

0	50	100	150	200 Miles
0	100	200	300 Km

Saladin attacks Krak, 1183

Saladin's invasion & defeat, 1177

Saladin's other campaigns, 1173-85

Reynald of Châtillon's capture of pilgrim caravan, 1181

Reynald of Châtillon's Red Sea expedition & defeat, 1182-3

Saladin's Empire by 1174

Muslim territory brought into Saladin's Empire after 1174

Regained by Saladin from Latins, 1170-86

Byzantine Empire

Cilician Armenia

Kingdom of Jerusalem

County of Tripoli

Principality of Antioch

ORIGINS OF THE CAMPAIGN

By the 1180s the realms carved out following the First Crusade were no longer real 'Crusader States', because the descendants of the First Crusaders were no longer striving to expand. Instead they were struggling to survive and to protect the Holy Places of Christianity from Muslim reconquest. Leadership was also passing to men who were working towards coexistence with the surrounding Muslim peoples.

The Kingdom of Jerusalem remained the most important of the Latin States in Syria and Palestine. Of the others the County of Edessa (Urfa) had already been reconquered by the Muslims, the Principality of Antioch had fallen under Byzantine influence and even the small County of Tripoli now resisted Jerusalem's suzerainty. In the early 1180s the Kingdom of Jerusalem had 400,000 to 500,0000 inhabitants, no more than 120,000 of whom were Latins (Christians of western European origin). The rest consisted of indigenous 'Oriental' Christians, Muslims, Jews and Samaritans. The balance of power between feudal lords and ruler in late 12th-century Jerusalem is not entirely clear, but in general it seems that the king and lesser aristocracy were losing out while the leading barons grabbed ever more control. Meanwhile the Military Orders (Templars and Hospitallers) were growing in power, being given more castles which only they seemed able to garrison effectively.

The defence of the Kingdom of Jerusalem was theoretically the responsibility of all western European Christians, yet in reality the Latin States had to rely on themselves after the fiasco of the Second Crusade in 1148. What its leaders now wanted were professional soldiers and financial support — not hordes of belligerent Crusaders who stirred up trouble then went home. Meanwhile the catastrophic Byzantine defeat by the Seljuq Turks at Myriokephalon in 1176, and a massacre of Latins in Constantinople eight years later, meant that help from the Byzantine Empire was an illusion. The Kingdom of Jerusalem also faced problems within its borders. Few Armenians settled in Palestine and the warlike Maronite Christians of the mountains lived away from the main centres of power while the majority of Syriac-Jacobite Christians remained deeply suspicious of the Latins. The Latins' adoption of some eastern habits of dress and cleanliness was superficial and the cultural gulf between Latins and locals remained unbridged until the end. Relations between the Latin States and neighbouring Muslim states remained rooted in war, lasting peace probably being impossible as each side clung to ideologies that could not accept the other's existence. Attitudes based on the easy victories of the First Crusade meant that the military élite of the Latin States was still hugely overconfident. This did wonders for their morale but would soon lead to military disaster. Yet elements of doubt were already creeping in, and the second half of the 12th century saw the building of many defensive castles.

The eastern frontier of the Kingdom of Jerusalem actually consisted of distinct sectors. In the north (the Litani valley) were some impressive castles. The central sector from Mount Hermon (Jabal al Shaykh) along the Golan Heights to the Yarmuk valley was supposedly shared with the rulers of Damascus. The Muslims thought this zone should extend as far as the Balqa hills around Amman but in fact the Latins dominated a fertile plateau between the River Yarmuk and the Ajlun hills. Southward again lay the Latin territory of Oultrejordain, lying between the River Jordan, Dead Sea and Wadi Araba in the west, and the strategic road from Amman to Aqabah. From Oultrejordain the Latins had levied tolls on Muslim traffic between Syria and Egypt, even on

Muslim *Haj* or Pilgrim caravans travelling south to Mecca and Medina. Then, in the early 1170s, Saladin's reconquest of territory south of Montreal (Shawbak) had a profound psychological impact, 'liberating the Haj Road' so that pilgrims, at least from Egypt, no longer paid humiliating tolls to the infidel.

The most striking development on the Muslim side of the frontier had been Saladin's unification of Islamic territory neighbouring the Latin States. Only in the far north did the Latins now have any neighbour other than Saladin, and that was the fellow Christian state of Cilician Armenia. Yet there had been other equally important changes in the Muslim Middle East. The concept of *jihad* as war against the infidel, long dormant, was revived by 12th-century Sunni Muslim scholars. *Jihads* became organized campaigns to recover the Holy Land, just as Crusades had been to conquer it. They were not, however, intended to convert the enemy by the sword since Islam has always frowned on forcible

▲ *Demons on carved capital from the Church of the Annunciation, Nazareth, late 12th century. They reflect the Latin image of their Muslim foes – leather shields, no body armour and with an emphasis on archery. (Plaster cast in Victoria & Albert Museum, London: author's photograph)*

conversion. Nevertheless the 12th century did see a hardening of religious attitudes, greater intolerance and increased pressure on indigenous Oriental Christians. This Sunni Muslim revival was also directed against the Shi'a Muslim minority.

The loss of Jerusalem to the Crusaders had actually increased the city's importance to Muslims, being followed by an outpouring of *fada'il* or 'praise literature' about the Holy City. The responsibilities of rulers were also described in a number of books known as 'Mirrors for Princes', and one of the most interesting was written by an anonymous Syrian living near the Crusader frontier a year or so after Saladin's

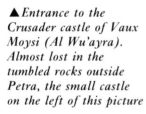
▲ *Entrance to the Crusader castle of Vaux Moysi (Al Wu'ayra). Almost lost in the tumbled rocks outside Petra, the small castle on the left of this picture* *relied on steep cliffs and clefts for its protection. The stone bridge spanning the chasm is modern. (Author's photograph)*

▲ *The ancient Roman city of Ba'albak in Lebanon was the centre of a strategic frontier governorate in Saladin's empire. Many ancient buildings were* *incorporated into its fortifications and new defences such as the Southern Tower on the right of this picture were added. (Author's photograph)*

death. It went into great detail about *jihad* and although the best *jihad* was still against evil in one's own heart, fighting the unbeliever came a good second. In fact the inhabitants of Syria's cities, particularly Aleppo in the north, had long traditions of scientific siege warfare and the 12th century saw the building of many new fortifications in Muslim Syria, just as it did in the Latin States. Meanwhile the Arab bedouin of the desert fringes remained strong but, having lost political dominance to the invading Turks, now generally preferred to be left alone. The people of Egypt, on the other hand, largely left warfare to their rulers, yet even here fundamental changes were taking place. The Arabization of the country

really started under the Fatimids who had ruled Egypt from AD 969, and the Arab bedouin of Egypt continued to prosper after Saladin seized control in 1171.

Islam's relations with Europe, rather than just the Latin States in Syria, were also changing. By the 12th century Muslim naval power in the Mediterranean was in steep decline while Italian merchant republics such as Pisa, Genoa and Venice controlled the sea lanes. Saladin would, in fact, be the last ruler of medieval Egypt to attempt a revival of Egyptian naval power — an attempt that ultimately failed. In the Red Sea, however, Egypt remained dominant, defeating Latin Crusader raids and piracy with relative ease.

Saladin's Empire in 1187

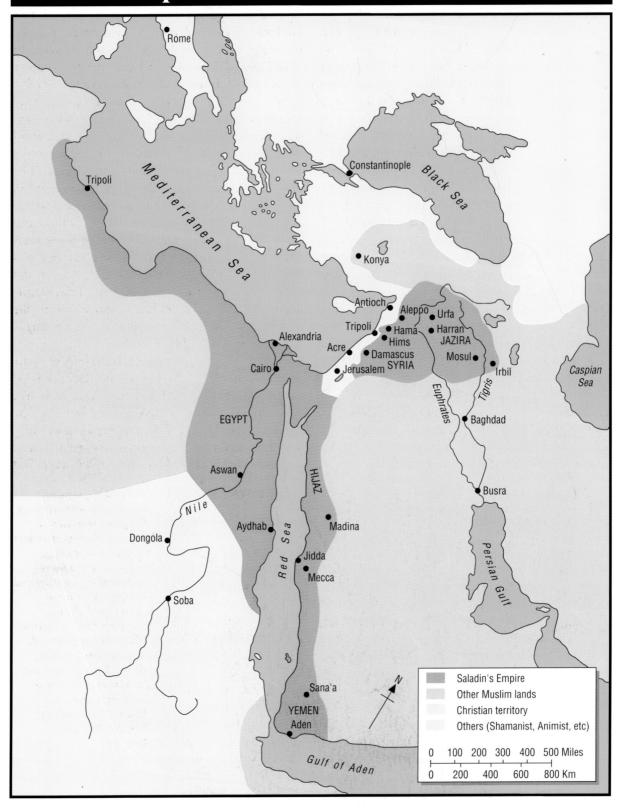

Rome

Tripoli

Mediterranean Sea

Constantinople

Black Sea

Konya

Antioch

Aleppo · Urfa
Tripoli · Hama · Harran
Acre · Hims · JAZIRA
Alexandria
Damascus
Jerusalem · SYRIA · Mosul
Cairo · Irbil

Caspian Sea

Euphrates

Tigris

Baghdad

EGYPT

Aswan

Busra

HIJAZ

Nile

Dongola

Aydhab · Madina

Red Sea

Jidda
Mecca

Persian Gulf

Soba

Sana'a

YEMEN
Aden

Gulf of Aden

N

	Saladin's Empire
	Other Muslim lands
	Christian territory
	Others (Shamanist, Animist, etc)

0   100   200   300   400   500 Miles
0   200   400   600   800 Km

Saladin's unification of so much of the Middle East took decades of war and diplomacy. From his power base in Egypt he and his family, the Ayyubids, won control of Yemen (1173), Damascus (1174) and Aleppo (1183). By 1186 Saladin also imposed his suzerainty over the Jazira (eastern Syria, south-eastern Turkey and northern Iraq), a rich region which provided a reservoir of military manpower. Overconfident the leaders of the Latin States may have been, but they watched the growth of Saladin's power with alarm and sent embassies to various parts of Europe seeking support. King Henry II of England had long been sympathetic, though his help took the form of cash rather than troops. A special tax in aid of Jerusalem had already been levied and in 1172, as part of his penance for the murder of Becket, Henry promised to support two hundred knights for one year in Jerusalem. Five years later he sent a chest of money to Jerusalem and in 1185 promised yet more. In fact these donations may have totalled 30,000 marks, a huge sum for those days and one that would play a crucial role in the forthcoming Hattin campaign.

Within the Latin States a census was conducted to discover their real military potential, while taxes were raised and castles strengthened. The strategic importance of Oultrejordain also increased now that Saladin controlled both Egypt and Syria. Here Reynald of Châtillon, who ran an effective intelligence service among the bedouin, planned to smash the Muslim ring surrounding the Latin States and perhaps even break into the Indian Ocean with its fabulous wealth of trade. In 1181-2 Reynald raided the Hijaz and the support he got from some local tribes clearly worried Saladin. Reynald's spectacular but disastrous naval expedition into the Red Sea the following year sent shock waves throughout the Islamic world and dented Saladin's status as Protector of the Muslim Holy Places in Mecca and Madina. The Sultan struck back immediately, and then again in 1183. In response the Christians fielded the largest army so far raised by the Latin States, but adopted a defensive stance by refusing to meet Saladin in a set-piece battle. This strategy was effective and the Muslims withdrew. Yet the invasion caused great damage and many people blamed Count Raymond, on whose advice the passive strategy had been adopted, for missing a chance to destroy Saladin.

Iron mines were almost as important as water sources and the Jabal Ajlun to the north of Oultrejordain had such mines. These hills had come under Saladin's control by 1184 and the Sultan sent Izz al Din Usamah, previously governor of the iron-rich mountains near Beirut, to build a new castle overlooking Ajlun itself. But

◀ Painted fragment from a mid 12th-century Egyptian manuscript showing Muslim warriors wearing full mail hauberks and turbans, supported by unarmoured infantry with large kite-shaped shields, emerging from a fortress to fight Crusaders. The Muslims are probably Fatimid troops and the fortress may represent Ascalon. (Dept. of Oriental Antiquities, British Museum, London)

◀ Qala'at al Rabadh outside Ajlun was built for Saladin in 1184-5. This picture, taken by a German aircraft on 9 April 1918, shows a small castle of rectangular plan. The four main towers date from Saladin's reign; some outer defences were added in the 13th century. (Royal Jordanian Geographical Centre)

although the Muslims were nibbling away at the Kingdom of Jerusalem, Saladin faced problems away in the east. A severe drought also struck Palestine in 1185 and so it was with some relief that both sides agreed to a four-year truce. This did not mean peace on all fronts, of course. In 1186 the Principality of Antioch raided its Christian neighbours in Cilicia while in south-eastern Anatolia a bloody struggle broke out between Kurds and Turcomans (nomadic Turks), both of whom were vital sources of military manpower for Saladin's armies. The Byzantine Empire was also wracked by dissention. Two leading noblemen, Isaac and Alexius Angelus, had sought refuge at Saladin's court but in 1185 Isaac Angelus returned to Constantinople, overthrew the Emperor Andronicus to become Byzantine Emperor himself. The following year his brother

Alexius was imprisoned in the Latin States as he made his way home. There were similar tensions on Saladin's eastern border. In 1180 the new Caliph Al Nasir had succeeded to the throne of Baghdad and under his energetic rule the once mighty Abbasid dynasty saw a final burst of glory. Yet Al Nasir's ambitions clashed with Saladin's plans in northern Iraq and relations between the two Muslim leaders were cool.

In Jerusalem the leper king, Baldwin IV, died in 1185 and in August 1186 his child successor Baldwin V also died, throwing the Kingdom into a major crisis. The Regent, Count Raymond of Tripoli, was ousted in a coup by a belligerent 'Court Party' who wanted a tougher policy towards the Muslims. They had Sibylla, sister of

Baldwin IV, crowned Queen and thus her husband, a French nobleman named Guy de Lusignan, became King. For months many Jerusalem nobles refused to recognize the coup — though in the end only Count Raymond continued to deny homage to King Guy. Instead Raymond retired to Tiberius, capital of the seigniory of Galilee which he held through his wife Eschiva of Galilee. Naturally Saladin watched this crisis with interest. He released some of Raymond's knights who had been prisoners of war and sent his own troops to support Raymond in Tiberius. For a while it looked as if King Guy would attack Raymond. Beyond Jerusalem Prince Raymond III of Antioch also refused to recognize Guy, though he would do so after war broke out with Saladin.

◄ *Heraldry was never as highly developed in the Muslim countries as in Europe, but emblems were used by some of Saladin's leading* amirs. *These confronted hawks over the entrance to Qala'at al Rabadh (far left) may have been the badge of Izz al Din Usamah who governed the castle for Saladin. Near left is another motif carved over a castle entrance, this one at Qala'at al Jindi in Sinai. The castle was completed for Saladin as the Hattin campaign was taking place. The same motif had also been seen on the Fatimid Bab al Nasr of Cairo built exactly a century earlier. (Author's photographs)*

► *Small carvings of soldiers around a highly decorated arch from Sinjar in north-western Iraq. It dates from the early 12th century and shows the weapons used by élite* mamluk *troops. (Iraqi National Museum, Baghdad)*

THE OPPOSING LEADERS

The Muslim Commanders

Saladin has traditionally been seen in Europe as a paragon of virtue and a hero. Recently, however, a critical view has portrayed him as an ambitious, ruthless and devious politician, and less brilliant as a commander than once thought. As usual the truth probably lies between these extremes, though all agree that Sultan Saladin was the greatest man in the history of the 12th-century Middle East. Saladin's family, the Ayyubids, was of Kurdish origin and had served Nur al Din, the Turkish ruler of Syria and northern Iraq. Saladin himself was educated and given military training in the cultivated surroundings of a Turkish court in Arabian Syria, though it was in Egypt that he rose to power. As a ruler he listened to advice, particularly on political matters, and made use of existing military structures as well as new ideas. Contemporary Muslim biographers tend to idealize his character, emphasizing his humanity, his forgiving nature, piety, love of justice, generosity, courage. They may have exaggerated but there is no doubt that Saladin made a

◄ *Early 13th-century ceramic bowl from Persia showing a Muslim ruler holding a* gurz *(mace). He is seated between two military leaders who wear full mail* dir' *(hauberks) beneath sleeveless surcoats. (Toledo Museum of Art, Ohio, Edward Drummond Libbey Gift)*

profound impact on those around him. Even his Christian foes trusted Saladin's honour.

Contrary to some romantic views, the Sultan was no military 'innocent' thrust into warfare against his will. He had had considerable experience as a staff officer under Nur al Din and fought in several battles before taking over as Vizier (Chief Minister) of Egypt in 1169. Saladin did not become titular ruler of that country until 1171, and even then Egypt theoretically remained part of Nur al Din's realm until the latter's death in 1173. As a commander Saladin was willing to take considerable risks and he had a clear understanding of broad strategy. On the other

▼1. Saladin. The Sultan is shown with a tall yellow cap beneath a white shawl. He wears a mail coif and a mail-lined kazaghand. His sword is the one attributed to Saladin in the Istanbul Army Museum. 2. Tawashi cavalryman. As one of the élite troops trained for close combat, this man's armour is as heavy as that of his Crusader foes. 3. Ayyubid guardsman. Ayyubid court costume reflected Persian and Turkish styles, hence he wears no armour. Illustrations by Angus McBride.

hand he made mistakes, for example allowing Latin resistance to crystalize at Tyre (Sur) after his overwhelming victory at Hattin.

Nevertheless Saladin remained the noble and tragic — though 'pagan' — hero of various European tales. His greatness was such that the Latins seemed unable to accept that he was a 'mere Saracen'. So legends grew up claiming that Saladin was the grandson of a beautiful French Princess forced to marry a valiant Turk named Malakin. He, it was said, '...lived long and tenderly with his wife. Neither were they childless, for of this lady, who was called the Fair Captive, was born the mother of that courteous Turk, the Sultan Saladin, an honourable, a wise and a conquering lord.'

Saladin had great respect for his nephew Taqi al Din who, like so many Islamic leaders of this period, was described by contemporary Muslim writers as deeply religious and very generous. This may have been true, but what comes across most clearly was his physical courage and preference for leading troops in person. Taqi al Din had demonstrated his initiative long before Hattin, his prompt action saving the day at the Battle of Hama (against the troops of Muslim Aleppo and Mosul) in 1175. Now Saladin gave him the toughest military tasks, often placing him in command of the right wing which, in the

▲ This early 13th-century carving over the Bab al Tillism gate of Baghdad was destroyed by an explosion in 1917. It showed a 'hero-ruler' in Turkish costume – *long plaits and rich tunic plus an elaborate turban – seizing two dragons. (Photograph via the Staatliche Museen zu Berlin)*

traditional tactics of the Middle East, usually took an offensive role while the left wing acted defensively.

In addition to being an outstanding commander, Taqi al Din was impetuous and obstinate. His political ambitions aimed at a power base larger than the central Syrian province of Hama which he had governed since 1178. Saladin was fully aware of the tempestuous Taqi al Din's desire for independence — perhaps seeing him as a kindred spirit — but the Sultan still made him governor of Egypt while he himself was away. Taqi al Din next dreamed of carving out a state in North Africa, but Saladin feared that he would take away too many valuable troops. Dismissed as governor of Egypt, he almost rebelled against Saladin and quarrelled openly with Saladin's son Al Afdal. Yet Saladin was soon reconciled with his warlike nephew, adding the mountainous frontier region around Mayyafariqin in Anatolia to Taqi al Din's existing Syrian fief of Hama. Here the young warrior had a chance to expand his territory without clashing with other members of the family. Even so Taqi al Din virtually deserted Saladin during the crisis of the Third Crusade, only to die suddenly a bare seventeen months before the great Sultan himself.

Muzaffar al Din Gökböri was one of Saladin's leading *amir*s or military commanders. Like all such *amir*s he governed large provinces from which he drew revenues to pay his troops. Gökböri, which means 'Blue Wolf' in Turkish, was a son of the governor of Irbil. His father had been a loyal follower of the great Zangi whose conquest of Edessa in 1144 was the first step in rolling back the Crusades. Gökböri himself served Zangi's son Nur al Din and became governor of Harran in what had been the Latin County of Edessa. In 1175 he led the right wing of a combined Aleppo-Mosul army against Saladin at the Horns of Hama, but after Nur al Din's death Zangi's dynasty was falling apart and a new Muslim hero arose — Saladin. Gökböri's defection to Saladin was a major factor in the Sultan's success. Yet it was also a dangerous move because if Saladin failed, Gökböri would lose everything. In the event Saladin defeated the remaining Zangids and added the cities of Edessa (Urfa) and Samsat to Gökböri's governorate. He also gave one of his sisters, Al Sitt Rabia Khatun, to the 'Blue Wolf' in marriage.

Gökböri's military skills were widely recognized, Saladin's secretary, the chronicler Al Isfahani, describing him as '...the audacious, the hero of well thought out projects, the lion who heads straight for the target, the most reliable and firmest chief'. He remained a leading *amir* after the Hattin campaign and though he had to give his original fiefs to Taqi al Din, he was compensated with his father's old governorate around Irbil. This he ruled until dying at the age of eighty-one. In Syria Gökböri was remembered as a great warrior, but in Irbil in what is now Iraqi Kurdistan the old Turk was remembered as a patron of scholars such as the historian Ibn Khallikan. He built colleges, hospitals, almshouses and hostels for pilgrims and merchants. Gökböri was also the first ruler to patronize the previously unofficial Mawlid al Nabi (Birthday of the Prophet Muhammad) festival, perhaps in imitation

of a large Christian community which then lived in Irbil. Only five years after his death the Mongols arrived, destroying Gökböri's cultural works, and all that seems to remain is the beautifully decorated brick minaret of Irbil's Old Mosque.

Little is known about the Hajib Husam al Din Lu'lu's background. He was almost certainly a *mamluk* as the name Lul'lu, meaning 'Pearl', was usually given to slaves. He may also have been of Armenian origin. Even his title of Hajib (Chamberlain) does not say much. Under the previous Fatimid rulers of Egypt, when Lu'lu may already have been a courtier, the Hajib was an important court official though not a military one. Under the Seljuqs of Iran the Hajib was a court official who could also lead armies.

According to one chronicler, Husam al Din Lu'lu was a *shaykh* or man of religion. But it was as commander of Saladin's fleet that he earned fame, defeating Reynald of Châtillon's audacious raid into the Red Sea in 1183 and personally leading marines in a naval battle which led to the capture of Gibelet (Jubayl) four years later. After taking a relief fleet to Acre in 1189 Lu'lu seems to disappear from the records. Was he among 2,700 men of Acre's garrison slaughtered on Richard the Lionheart's orders in 1191? A senior officer named Husam al Din was still in Al Adil's service in 1194, but there is no certainty that he was the same man.

Whether or not Lu'lu died at Acre, retired after the destruction of the Egyptian Mediterranean fleet at Acre, or went on to serve Al Adil, he had already won enough fame to be included alongside Saladin in a panegyric by the poet Ibn al Dharawil. Saladin's secretary Al Isfahani, was also full of praise for Lu'lu, '...whose courage was well known to the infidels, whose violence against the enemy was extolled. He was without equal when it came to raids with which none but he were associated... happy in all he undertook, agreeable in character.' Ibn al Athir, a less flowery chronicler, simply described Husam al Din Lu'lu as '...an emir known for his bravery, prudence and good humour' and as '... a brave and energetic man, a naval and military expert full of useful initiative'.

The Christian Commanders

Most of the original sources are unsympathetic to Guy, King of Jerusalem (1186-92), as the ruler who lost Jerusalem to the Muslims. Guy and his French knights were also disliked by the local Latin aristocracy. He was clearly handsome and won the heart of Queen Sibylla of Jerusalem, but whether he was as weak and frivolous as most chroniclers suggest is less certain. He emerges as a far more decisive character after Hattin than before it. Traditional historians still describe Guy as an ineffective *bailli* (Regent) during the crisis of 1183 and as being tight with money even before

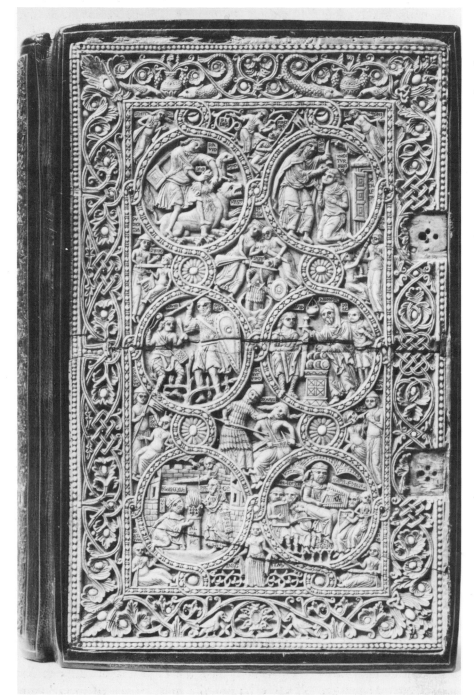

◀ *The ivory cover of Queen Melisende's Psalter, made in Jerusalem AD 1131-43. It symbolizes the King of Jerusalem's claim to rule as King David's successor. The warriors reflect Byzantine or Islamic arms and armour, particularly 'Fortitude' who slays 'Avarice' below and to the right of 'David and Goliath'. (British Museum, London)*

he became king. The late R.C. Smail, however, gives Guy some credit for forcing Saladin's withdrawal in 1183. On the other hand he does appear to have been easily influenced by friends who offered conflicting and not always sound advice. As a result King Guy tended to change his mind at crucial moments.

Of course the basis of Guy's authority was weak, as the laws of the Kingdom of Jerusalem reflected a European ideal of 'constitutional' feudal monarchy rather than the reality of conditions in the Latin States. Even Guy's command of the army was rather theoretical and he constantly had to consult his barons and other men before issuing an order. Confusion, resentment, jealousy and insubordination were rife throughout the Kingdom and Guy could rarely impose effective discipline. On the other hand his final decisions and the tactics he adopted, even at Hattin, were fully in line with the accepted strategy of the time — a strategy which had served the Latin States well in the past.

In many ways Count Raymond III of Tripoli was the most tragic figure in the whole Hattin saga. Perhaps the most intelligent of Latin leaders, he often tried to achieve peaceful coexistence with neighbouring Muslim rulers. He also emerged as the best tactician among the Kingdom of Jerusalem's military leaders. Yet in the end Raymond was branded a traitor, as the man responsible for Christian defeat by Saladin, and he retired to die a broken man within a few months of that catastrophe.

Raymond became Count of Tripoli at the age of only twelve, after his father was killed by Isma'ili 'Assassins'. By 1175 his ability and experience had made him leader of the local barons and he was later the natural choice to be Regent, ruling the Kingdom of Jerusalem in the name of the dying leper King Baldwin IV. In this role Raymond showed himself patient, careful and ingenious in dealing with various factions in the Kingdom and with its neighbours. The calculating Count Raymond was also capable of adapting to a changing situation; an adaptability rare among his hidebound contemporaries in Jerusalem. Eight years as a prisoner in Aleppo had made him fluent in Arabic and given him considerable knowledge

of Islam, plus a certain admiration rather than hatred for his captors. Unlike newly arrived Crusaders, Raymond no longer saw the Muslims merely as foes but as neighbours — though rivals — with a shared interest in the harvest, the uncertain rainfall and in trade. For their part the Muslims regarded Raymond III of Tripoli as the bravest as well as the shrewdest of Latin leaders. But when the final crisis came he fought as hard as any to save the Kingdom and if Guy had followed Raymond's advice the Battle of Hattin might have been avoided or even won.

Of all the leading characters in the story of the loss of Jerusalem, none is more colourful than Reynald. The traditional view portrays him as a recklessly brave, handsome but undisciplined adventurer who came to the Latin States in 1153 without wealth or followers yet won the hand of the young Princess Constance of Antioch. Unscrupulous and brutal he may have been, but Reynald had an astonishing grasp of geopolitical strategy. Unfortunately for the Kingdom of Jerusalem, his vision far outstripped the military or economic capabilities of the Latin States. Unlike Raymond of Tripoli, who had also spent years as a prisoner among the Muslims, Reynald's captivity in Aleppo (1161-75) had left him with a burning hatred for Islam — though also a great knowledge of its geography. He emerged as a fanatical Crusader. The Muslims in turn well knew that 'Arnat', as they called him, was their most dedicated foe.

By the time of Reynald's release, his wife Constance had died and so, without delay, Reynald married the heiress to Krak (Karak) and thus became master of the great seigniory of Oultrejordain. Here he gradually built up a state-within-a-state, perhaps one day hoping to make it an independent lordship like the County of Tripoli or the Principality of Antioch.

Balian, the Lord of Rama (Ramlah), came from the most famous feudal family in the Latin Kingdom of Jerusalem. Yet this d'Ibelin family had humble origins, being part of a 'new aristocracy' which rose from the rank-and-file of knights who carved out the Kingdom in the early 12th century. By the 1180s Balian d'Ibelin had become one of the most respected local barons

◀ *Twelfth-century 'Exultet Roll' from Benevento in southern Italy, showing a king giving military authority to the commander of his guards, or* protospatharius *in the Byzantine-Greek term used here. The costumes and weaponry reflect a mixture of Western, Byzantine and Islamic styles, perhaps similar to those found in the Latin States of the Middle East. (Biblioteca Casanatense, Ms. 724. B1. 13, Rome; N. Murgioni photograph)*

◀ *Late 12th to early 13th-century stucco relief from Persia showing horsemen fighting with spears held in both hands. They wear lamellar* jawshan *(cuirasses), that on the right having flaps to protect the upper arms. (Museum of Art, Seattle)*

and enjoyed semi-autonomous authority in the south of Palestine. Trusted by all sides, he had acted as an intermediary in negotiations between King Guy and Count Raymond of Tripoli. Balian was also well known as a negotiator among the Muslims and was counted a personal friend by Saladin himself.

Nevertheless Balian remained a convinced Christian and a dedicated defender of the Kingdom. Released by Saladin after Hattin, he swore never again to take arms against the Sultan. Yet Balian d'Ibelin allowed himself to be absolved from this oath by the Patriarch of Jerusalem and took command of the Holy City's defences where he showed enormous courage and determination. It says a great deal for the respect between Balian and Saladin, qualities that bridged the religious divide, that the Sultan could understand Balian's oath-breaking and forgive him when Jerusalem finally fell on 2 October 1187.

THE OPPOSING ARMIES

Saladin's Forces: Recruitment

Medieval Muslim armies were highly organized compared to their Crusader enemies and some aspects of their structure, tactics and traditions went back to the ancient Romano-Byzantine or Persian Empires. Warfare was largely left to professional soldiers although religious volunteers did play a role against the invading Crusaders. Possession of a horse also gave status in medieval Islamic society, as it did in Europe. On the other hand the élite of the Muslim countries had lived in towns since at least the 9th century, rather than in scattered castles like the feudal aristocracy of the West. Regular soldiers also dwelt within the city walls, though irregulars camped outside. Turks and Kurds who formed the bulk of such professionals were rough compared to the cultured Arab emirs of the old Fatimid regime, while the sophisticated urban populations regarded them as a barbarous but necessary addition to their streets. Such men often came from long-standing military families in which young warriors acquired experience of leadership and tactics fighting alongside their relatives. Unlike the fully professional *mamluk*s of slave origin, such free-born warriors often had other activities including trades to keep them busy in time of peace. Among those who rose high in Muslim armies were men of humble birth, but in Saladin's day most leaders were drawn from free-born soldiers rather than the slave-recruited *mamluk*s.

The proportion of various ethnic groups within 12th-century Islamic armies is not easy to judge, as the origins of leaders did not necessarily reflect the men they led. Saladin's armies grew out of those of his Zangid predecessors and, like all the states which emerged from the fragmentation of the Great Seljuq empire in the early 12th century, the Zangids were highly militarized and looked east for cultural, political and military inspiration. The force which Nur al Din sent to Egypt in 1169, in which Saladin served as a staff officer, consisted of 6,000 Turcomans, 2,000 Kurds and a tiny élite of 500 *mamluk*s. It was around this force that Saladin built his own army when he took over Egypt a few years later. At first he also used some of the old Fatimid regiments but most of these were disbanded within a short while.

In Syria and the Jazira region Saladin made a policy of trying to recruit the troops of defeated Muslim rivals. The loyalty of those who did join him was strengthened by flattering their sense of *asabiyah* (family pride) and Saladin's armies soon proved that they had greater experience as well as better discipline than Muslim forces from eastern Anatolia or Persia. As Saladin's authority spread, so regional armies grew up under various provincial governors. Their recruitment often differed from that of the Sultan's own forces. Aleppo relied primarily on Turcoman tribes such as the Yürük, Damascus recruiting Arab tribesmen from central Syria, and Kurds playing a prominent role around Mosul. Nevertheless, the core of most such forces remained slave-recruited *mamluk*s. Fiercely loyal to the man who had bought, educated and then freed them, such warriors had formed the bodyguards of Abbasid Caliphs for centuries. Now Saladin combined the old Abbasid and newer Fatimid practices, mostly buying slaves of pagan Turkish origin from Asia. This élite joined the Sultan's guard which also looked after the main arsenals, garrisoned important fortifications and were stationed in the centre of Saladin's army in battle.

The largest ethnic group in the army was that of the Turks who had been the dominant military element in Syria since the early 12th century. Some tribes had migrated into northern Syria in

▶ *Painted panels from Capella Palatina, Palermo. Near right, an Arab cavalryman with a spear and long kite-shaped shield. Another horseman below is indulging in the universal aristocratic pastime of hawking. Far top right, an Arab warrior with a spear and small round shield, riding a camel, c. 1140. Such troops served as auxiliaries in Saladin's army, but this man appears on a panel painted in Islamic style for the Norman rulers of Sicily. Far below right, an Arab horseman with a spear and fur-trimmed hat. (Author's photographs)*

◀ **Left: The equipment of a poorer knight differed in quality and amount from that of a rich knight. His helmet has an old-fashioned nasal and he carries a massive shield for infantry combat, perhaps for attacking a castle. Right: A new feature in 12th-century armour were mailed mittens and mail chausses for the legs. Some helmets were also given a fixed face-guard. Under his hauberk this knight wears a padded** akton **or gambeson. Illustrations by Angus McBride.**

the 1120s but the majority of Turkish troops were still recruited from Turcoman tribes in the Diyarbakr region. Second in numerical importance were the Kurds who fought as cavalry and archers, though apparently they were not using the horse-archery tactics of their Turkish rivals. Saladin recruited them either as individuals or as whole units from various tribes, such tribal units generally fighting as one block in battle. A third important ethnic element were the Arabs. There had been a resurgence of nomadism in northern Syria following a Byzantine military revival of the 11th century. But although these Arab nomads were rich in horses they had few archers, fighting instead with spear or sword. Nevertheless the bedouin continued to supply vital auxiliary cavalry to the rulers of 12th-century Syria — though they were deeply mistrusted by the settled Arab peasantry and city dwellers. Such bedouin featured in Saladin's army as *qufl*, infantry raiders who specialized in harassing an enemy's communications, and as *lisus* , cavalry infiltrators whose role was to interrupt enemy supplies.

The *muttawiyah* or religious volunteers often served for very short periods, but they could be quite effective, particularly when harassing enemy stragglers. Unlike the *ahdath* (urban militias), the true religious volunteers were difficult for a government to control. Meanwhile the *ahdath* tended to be recruited from the poorer sections of city populations. By the 12th century its main duty was to police a city or town, though it could also fight alongside the regular army in an emergency. Under Fatimid rule the *ahdath* of Palestinian towns may have included Jews as well as Muslims, but whether this was true of Saladin's *ahdath* is not known. Other local troops included the often despised *rajjalah* infantry. Specialist infantry would have been professionals, even if part-time, and the wealthy city of Aleppo was famous for warriors who also seem to have had a well-developed sense of humour. Back in 1071, when the Saljuq Turks were attacking Aleppo, the defenders wrapped a bale of silk around their strongest tower and sent a message to the enemy saying that the Turks' stone-throwing machines had given it a headache! Aleppo was still famous for its miners and siege engineers in Saladin's day, while the garrison of Aleppo's citadel were also looked after by a professional government-paid doctor. Engineers from far away Khurasan may have served Saladin, and the Sultan was certainly delighted to get a squad of specialist fire-troops from the Abbasid Caliph of Baghdad. Meanwhile North Africa played its part by supplying naval crews, of which Saladin was always short, the Maghribis (North Africans) being regarded as the best sailors in the Muslim World.

Organization of Saladin's Forces

Saladin's army was subdivided into units of various sizes, though the terms used often overlapped. The smallest were the *jarida* (70 men) and the *tulb* (70-200 men) with their own flag and trumpeter. The *jama'a* was probably a tactical formation consisting of three *jaridas*. The *sariya* was an *ad hoc* band of about 20 cavalry, often used in ambushes, while the *saqa* was a small advance guard or reconnaissance party. Unlike their Latin foes the Muslims also had specific *amir* (officer) ranks, ranging from an *isfahsalar* (army leader) down through the ustadh al dar and *hajib* (chamberlain) senior commanders, to the *amir hajib*, *amir jandar*, *khazindar* (governor of an important citadel), *amir kabir* (great officer) and

◀ *Top left, back of a 12th-century bronze mirror from Persia showing a horseman using a couched lance to fight wild beasts. He also carries a large round shield. (Louvre Museum, Paris)*

◀ *Top right: this magnificent late 12th- to early 13th-century ceramic statuette of a horseman fighting a giant serpent stands about one metre high and comes from Raqqa in north-eastern Syria. The man wears a segmented helmet, wields a straight broad sword and carries*

a small typically Turkish round qalqan *shield made of woven cane and cotton. (Syrian National Museum, Damascus)*

◀ *Below, 'Rabi in combat with Warqa's father', in the late 12th- to early 13th-century* Warqa wa Gulshah *manuscript. It was probably painted in Azarbayjan and illustrates the arms, armour and costume of the Saljuq Turkish aristocracy of much of the Middle East. (Topkapi Library, Istanbul, Ms. Haz. 841)*

ordinary *amir*. A *ra'is* headed the *ahdath* militia while the *shihna* was chief of police. Regular soldiers were paid regular *jamakiyah* (salaries) or held *iqta* (land-grants), which had features in common with European feudal fiefs. The pay structure was controlled by a *Diwan al Jaysh* (Army Ministry). This *Diwan al Jaysh* also listed the troops' names, where they were stationed and held reviews to check training and equipment. Registered soldiers received weapons from government arsenals free, but if they lost this equipment the cost was deducted from their pay.

Any changes of rank, status or unit were also noted on the registers.

The *iqta* or fief was vital to this military system. It was really a system of tax-farming in which the holder took a proportion of revenues in return for ensuring that taxes were collected. One vital characteristic that distinguished an *iqta* from a European feudal fief was that the land could be taken back at any time. In return for an *iqta* the *muqta* (land-holder) also maintained and equipped a specified number of troops. Some *iqta*s were huge estates given to members of the ruling

◀ *Jarwajaraya infantry auxiliary. As a volunteer this man's weaponry is simple and his costume is that of a civilian, while most volunteers would lack swords. One javelin is designed to penetrate armour, and his shield is of the infantry januwiyah type. Illustration by Angus McBride.*

▲ *Smaller ceramic statuettes of armed horsemen come from late 12th- to early 13th-century Persia. This example carries a mace, has a shield on his back and a trained hunting cat riding behind his saddle. (Metropolitan Museum of Art, New York; author's photograph)*

family. Others were governorships of towns, castles and strategic districts bestowed on senior officers. Then there were villages and smaller estates given to lesser *amir*s. Salaries or pensions drawn from government properties could also be *iqta*s. The value of land-grants varied considerably, even within a single region. Only a generation after Saladin's death a survey showed *iqta*s ranging from one maintaining 250 horsemen, to another that included the towns of Nablus and Jinin supporting 120 horseman, to a small *iqta* maintaining 70 horsemen. Inferior land went as *iqta*s to *ajnad* militia or bedouin auxiliaries. Yet the *Muqta*s only lived on these estates if they had fallen from political favour.

Among various categories of troops the slave-recruited *mamluk*s generally formed a ruler's élite *askar* bodyguard. Fiercely disciplined and proud of its status, an *askar* also looked after siege engines, arsenals and other vital facilities. The *halqa* seems to have been a larger formation, perhaps comparable to a household regiment. The *tawashiya* included, by Saladin's day, both *mamluk*s and freely recruited cavalrymen, each

▶ *Two warriors on a mid 13th-century tile from Kashan in Persia. The man in front carries a small round shield, the man behind is wielding a spear with both hands. (Museum of Oriental Art, Rome, inv. 1056; author's photograph)*

▶ *Arab bedouin warrior stopping a fight between two travellers. This example of the* **Maqamat** *of Al Hariri was made in Mosul in 1256 and shows the very long spear characteristic of Arab horsemen. (British Library, Ms. Or. 1200, London)*

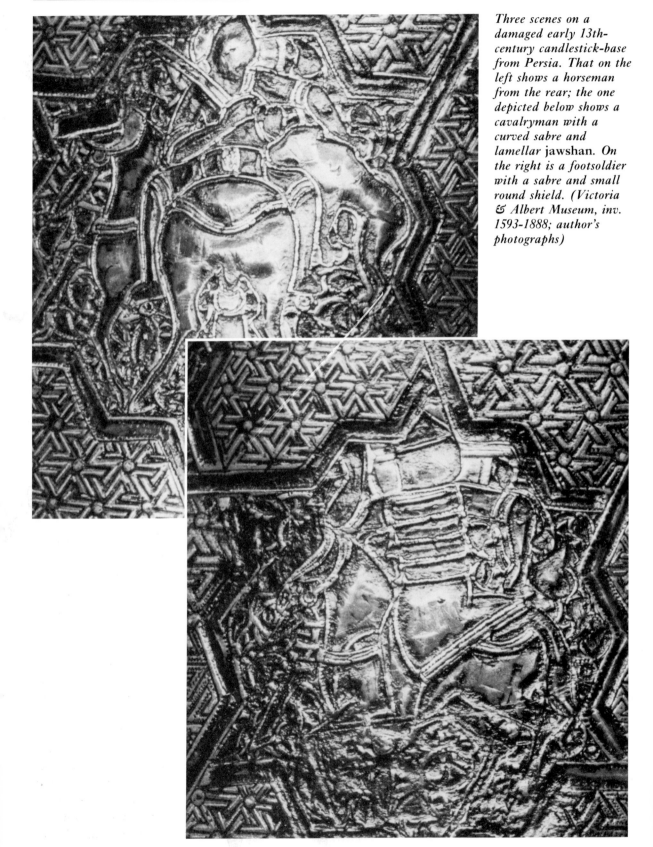

Three scenes on a damaged early 13th-century candlestick-base from Persia. That on the left shows a horseman from the rear; the one depicted below shows a cavalryman with a curved sabre and lamellar jawshan. *On the right is a footsoldier with a sabre and small round shield. (Victoria & Albert Museum, inv. 1593-1888; author's photographs)*

with his own horse, page or *mamluk* follower, about ten animals to carry baggage, and a salary to purchase equipment. Organized into first-rate regiments which remained close to the ruler on campaign, each *tawashi* was expected to serve in the army for a certain number of months every year. Men of the *ajnad* or territorial army had lower status but were still properly equipped cavalry though few seem to have been trained horse-archers. The infantry had even lower status, despite their essential role in siege warfare. Most were archers, crossbowmen, or fought with spear and shield. The *janib* may have operated as mobile mounted infantry, sometimes riding mules, but the only real élite among foot soldiers were the *nafatin* (fire-troops). All professional foot soldiers were paid salaries, at least while on campaign. The same was probably true of siege engineers such as the *naqqabun* (miners or engineers), *hajjarun* (masons) and *najjarun* (carpenters).

It was the support services, however, that really set this army apart from its Latin enemies. Considerable emphasis was put on good communications; a government *barid* (postal service) used carrier pigeons and couriers, while beacons could carry warnings from the frontiers at extraordinary speed. Equally important was the distribution of weapons. Most cities had arms bazaars and many, like Aleppo, Damascus, Cairo and Mosul, had their own weapons-manufacturing quarters. Arms were issued to the troops from the *zardkhanah* (arsenal) at the start of a campaign. On the march, however, armour and most weaponry would remain in the *thuql* (baggage train). This made the troops light and fast moving but could be disastrous if intelligence failed and there was a surprise attack. Consequently the *thuql* was commanded by an experienced and reliable *amir*. The *thuql* also incorporated fire-troops, blacksmiths to repair weapons, siege equipment with engineers and surveyors. Non-combattants in the *thuql* included servants, horse handlers, mule and donkey drivers, cameleers, scribes, religious functionaries, doctors and surgeons. The sophisticated medical services formed, in fact, a mobile hospital. The division of booty had always been carefully regulated in Muslim armies; one-fifth going to the government and the rest being distributed among the troops. Much would then be sold to the merchants of the *suq al 'askar* (soldiers' bazaar) which formed part of the baggage train. This *suq al 'askar* also supplied additional weaponry and other military supplies when needed.

Physical appearance, costume and a rudimentary form of heraldry distinguished individuals and groups within Saladin's military. While the Ayyubid family and the Turks wore their hair long, the Arabs with the possible exception of the bedouin shaved their heads. Almost all Muslim men had beards or moustaches, Saladin's sailors having to shave in order to pass themselves off as Crusaders when slipping through a Latin blockade. A tall yellow cap called a *kalawta* was used by the Ayyubids while Central Asian Turkish forms of wrap-around tunic also became popular in the ruling class. A *hiyasa* (belt) made of linked metal plates actually distinguished the élite while officers wore the *sharbush*, a stiff fur-trimmed cap with a raised front. A band of richly embroidered *tiraz* fabric bearing an inscription had long been given by rulers to their followers as a mark of allegiance. Inscriptions also appeared on shields in the 11th century and would become more common later. Other devices and colours indicated Iranian influence, perhaps via the widely popular *Shahnamah* (epic poem), but there would be no real system of Islamic heraldry until the Mamluk dynasty of the mid-13th century onwards. Devices remained personal, not hereditary, and there was never a governing body to regularize 'heraldry' as in Europe.

Taqi al Din's personal flag was described by a Crusader witness as looking like a pair of trousers, but what the ignorant European probably saw was either a doubled 'windsock' banner such as had been used by Turks and Persians for hundreds of years, or a flag bearing the double-bladed 'Sword of Ali' or a Turkish tribal *tamga* device. Taqi al Din's troops certainly marched beneath a yellow banner, yellow being the Ayyubids' favoured colour. It was not, however, one of the normal colours of Islamic symbolism (green, white, black, red) having been regarded with some disfavour in earlier years. While Arabs and Kurds used various types of flag, the Turks also held *tuq* or horsetail standards aloft.

Tactics of the Muslim Forces

Saladin continued to use the age-old *razzia* raiding tactics of the Arab Middle East though there had been a change in the way these were carried out. The old mixed infantry and cavalry armies now gave way to smaller élites of *mamluk* horse-archers supported by auxiliary cavalry using Turkish tactics of rapid manoeuvre, dispersal and harassment. Military manuals from the Islamic Middle Ages may reflect theory rather than reality, but the organizing of a battle array, an encampment, line of march, siege or counter-siege were very similar in works from the Fatimid, Ayyubid or even Mamluk periods. Saladin's siege tactics were almost entirely the same as those of his Fatimid predecessors, while his cavalry tactics were far more flexible than those of the Crusaders. Saladin's horsemen would even, if the situation were suitable, stand against a full-scale charge by the enemy's knights. Considerable skills were, in fact, demanded of a late 12th-century cavalryman. Literary sources give primacy to the spear, which could be wielded with one or both hands, thrust at the foe's arms or legs as well as his body. Once lances were broken horsemen drew their swords. Only in specifically Turkish sources are bows given much prominence.

Cavalry manuals written a generation or so later deal with the initiating and maintaining of an attack, feigning retreat, wheeling around in battle, evading the enemy and renewing an attack. Horse-archers are instructed how to control their mounts and how to shoot. The advantages of various forms of bow and arrow, as well as the use of thumbguards for long-distance shooting, are all discussed. So is the use of the javelin from horseback. The training of foot soldiers received less attention, but manuals did give advice for infantry archers, describing the skills they needed to fight in the open. A little later military experts were suggesting that infantry must be able to march long distances, recognize dangerous enemy formations that indicated an impending attack, know how to take cover, check and chase cavalry, and how to scatter or scare an enemy's horses.

Once in enemy territory any force should always keep its escape route open. This was particularly true of lightly equipped raiding parties whose function was to sow confusion and fear among the enemy. Arab bedouin auxiliaries excelled in setting ambushes, particularly if they were natives of the area. If a raid were to be made at night, cloudy, windy and rainy weather was best. If the enemy were strong, it was advisable to attack him just before dawn while he was still confused and sleepy. Set-piece battles were generally avoided but when they did take place it is difficult to tell how far the tactics of Saladin's day really followed the theories.

The *jandariyah* guard remained with the ruler and though Saladin normally placed his best *halqa* regiments in the centre, *halqa* troops also operated as independent formations. Heavy cavalry were certainly used in the charge, operating much like

▶ *Turcoman cavalry auxiliary. This tribesman wears a typical Turkish double-breasted coat over a mail hauberk and has the fur-lined hat of the tribal élite. His bow includes a* majra *(arrow-guide for shooting short darts). Illustration by Angus McBride.*

◀ Carved 11th- to 12th-century relief from the window of a mosque in Kubachi, Daghestan. Only in such isolated Turkish areas could one find representational sculpture on an Islamic religious building. This portrays a horse-archer with a typically Turkish Central Asian form of box-like quiver on his right hip. (Metropolitan Museum of Art, New York; author's photograph)

◀ A late 12th- to early 13th-century lustre plate from Persia showing a soldier carrying a tall shield the base of which is flattened. Such januwiyah, or mantlets, were specifically for infantry use. The man's turban and the hilt of his straight sword represent styles known in the Islamic Middle East long before the coming of the Saljuq Turks. (Keir College, London, inv. 151)

◄ 'Iranian army leaving the castle of Furud', scene from the Shahna-mah on a broken early 13th-century tile from Persia. Four warriors have helmets with extended neck-protections. The leading horseman wears a mail hauberk, the second carries a massive **gurz** (mace). In the rear-right one man carries two furled banners while another beats upon drums carried by a mule. (Museum of Fine Arts, Boston; author's photograph)

▶ A unique fragment of a late 12th- to 13th-century ceramic bowl from Egypt showing a Muslim horseman wearing kalsat al zard (mail leggings) and a mail hauberk. (Benaki Museum, Athens, inv. 391)

◀ 'Defending a castle' in a Mozarabic manuscript from Catalonia written in about 1100. It provides one of the clearest representations of a lu'ab, the smallest form of man-powered stone-throwing mang-onel, widely used in both Muslim and Christian Spain and in the Middle East. (Biblioteca Nazionale, Turin, inv. J. II. l, ff.189v-190r)

▶ A soldier with a turban and a straight sword, probably hung from a baldric rather than a belt. He appears in a medical manuscript written in Iraq in AD 1224. (Freer Gallery of Art, Washing-ton, inv. 575121; author's photograph)

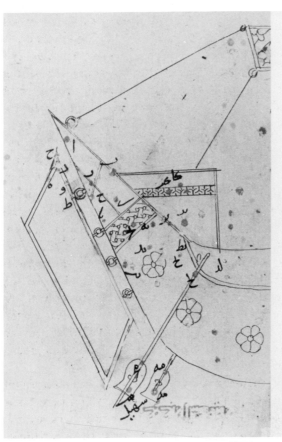

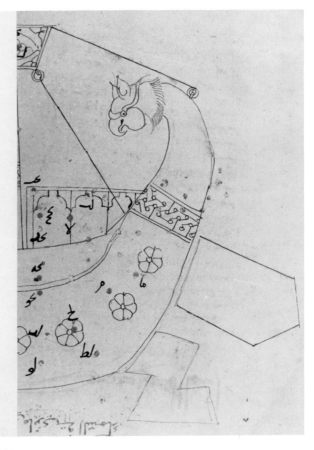

and Saladin used a *tal* (artificial hill of debris from long habitation, typical of the Middle East) to hide his reserves. But such sophisticated battlefield tactics demanded reliable battlefield communications and here the Muslims were well served by musical instruments, flags and *jawush* or *munadi* 'criers'.

Siege warfare was the main purpose of large expeditions. Lightly armed troops would be the first to reach and invest an enemy castle. The attackers would then protect their position with palisades before digging entrenchments. Siege towers might be built and miners would start undermining the enemy's walls. Mining operations, which demanded skilled personnel and careful direction, were in fact used by the Muslims more than by the Crusaders. In addition to battering rams the Muslims had a variety of stone-throwing engines, some of which were large enough to damage a wall or at least the battlements which gave cover to the defenders. The numerous smaller engines were essentially anti-personnel weapons designed to clear defenders from their positions prior to a general assault. One of the attackers' most important tasks was to protect their wooden siege engines and mines from defenders who might make a sortie. Once a breach had been made or a wall undermined, the garrison would be given an opportunity to surrender. If this were refused assault parties would be organized under the best available officers. When these managed to seize the breach they might again stop while the enemy was offered a final chance to surrender. Sieges could go on for months and in such cases the besiegers' camp could turn into a temporary town. Outside Acre in 1190 Saladin's position had 7,000 shops including 140 farriers, all controlled by a police force. Several markets included those for clothing and weaponry old or new, plus an estimated 1,000 small bath-houses mostly managed by North Africans. The contrast with the stinking disease-ridden camps of the Crusaders could hardly be more striking.

Muslim armies were just as sophisticated in defence of fortifications, most of which were based on long-established designs going back to the pre-Islamic period. The *burj* or tower was basic to

Latin knights, and, like knights, were divided into small *tulb* squadrons. Yet horse-archery remained the cavalry's most effective tactic. At long distance it could disrupt enemy formations by wounding horses and infantry. At close range the Muslims' composite bow could penetrate most 12th-century armour. Islamic infantry may have declined in importance since the 11th century but they still appeared in major set-piece battles as well as siege warfare. Although infantry were dismissed by many Muslim chroniclers as *harafisha* (rabble), Saladin's tactics often relied on separating an enemy's infantry from his cavalry even when fighting fellow Muslims. Terrain would be used to full advantage. Shirkuh lured Latin cavalry into an impossible charge up a slope of soft sand in 1167

◄ *'Argo' from a* **Suwar al Kawakib** *(Book of Constellations) made, probably in Egypt, in 1130-1. The mast and central part of the hull have been lost on later rebinding, but the ship clearly has a hinged* stern-rudder —*though the artist still had to include a pair of steering oars as these formed part of the star-pattern. (Topkapi Library, Istanbul, Ms. Ahmad III 3498, ff. 130v-131r)*

Islamic military architecture. Covered galleries along the top of a wall were also widespread while city walls tended to be high rather than thick. Major architectural changes appeared early in the 13th century as a result of the invention of the counterweight *mangonel*, but these had not appeared by Saladin's time. Garrisons included masons, sappers, crossbow-men, javelin-throwers, fire-troops and operators of stone-throwing machines. If an attack were imminent troops should pollute all the neighbouring water sources, and even attempt to spread disease downwind with the aid of carcasses. If possible the attackers should themselves be attacked by the garrison before they could establish their camp. Once the siege had begun the defenders must make night sorties to burn the enemy's machines, but if a sortie were attempted in daylight it could be in a strictly disciplined square formation.

Many of these ideas were used in naval warfare. Nevertheless the main role of Saladin's fleet was to transport troops rapidly from Egypt to Syria, and to hamper traffic between the Latin States and Europe. Marines would sail aboard

◀ *The basic plan of Aleppo's Citadel has not changed since the 12th or even 10th centuries though the present walls were strengthened in the 16th century. Towering above is the minaret of the Great Mosque built by Saladin's son Al Zahir Ghazi. (Author's photograph)*

▶ *Top: the walls of Cairo's Citadel looking south from the Burj al Ramla to the Burj al Imam, both built between 1183 and 1207. (Author's photograph)*

◀ *The 12th-century northern walls of Damascus follow the line of the 3rd-century Roman defences. This section overlooking the River Barada between the Bab Tuma and Bab al Salam gates has no towers. Towers are, however, regularly spaced around the eastern, southern and western walls of the city. (Author's photograph)*

▶ *Interior of a defensive chamber within the Burj al Ramla of Cairo's Citadel, built towards the end of Saladin's reign. (Author's photograph)*

larger merchant ships as well as fighting galleys and could include archers, fire-troops and operators of stone-throwing machines as well as boarders. When faced with an enemy fleet Muslim galleys made use of crescent-shaped or compacted formations, feigned retreat and used coastal features for cover. Although Muslim naval power had been in decline for more than a century, a naval manual of the 13th century could still claim that the Muslims were superior to Byzantines in naval warfare — but made no comparison with the now dominant Italian fleets. Saladin's ships were essentially the same as those of his enemies. A *shini* was the standard fighting galley, but many cargo vessels were also powered by oars. Others, of course, relied on sails and it is now known that three-masted ships were built by Muslim Mediterranean shipwrights more than a century before they reappeared in Christian fleets. As early as AD 955 one great ship was 95 metres long and almost 40 metres broad. The warships built in sections in Egypt and then transported across Sinai on camel-back to the Gulf of Aqabah in 1170 must, however, have been small. Other Indian Ocean vessels could be astonishingly large. Here there was less use of oars, partly because of reliable monsoon winds but more importantly because water sources were scarce and so smaller crews were an advantage. The hinged stern rudder, a Chinese invention, was also known to eastern Arabian sailors by at least the early 12th century.

Muslim Weapons

Saladin rose to power in the central regions of the Muslim World which were acutely short of iron and of fuel for working metals. The nearest important source of iron ore was eastern Anatolia, but otherwise Saladin's empire had to rely on imported ingots plus small mines in the mountains near Beirut and around Ajlun - both of which virtually straddled the frontier with the Latin States. Not surprisingly long-distance trade in pig-iron and refined steel, much from India, was vital for Saladin's armies. Despite such difficulties Egypt already had three state arsenals under the Fatimids, one employing 3,000 craftsmen, which

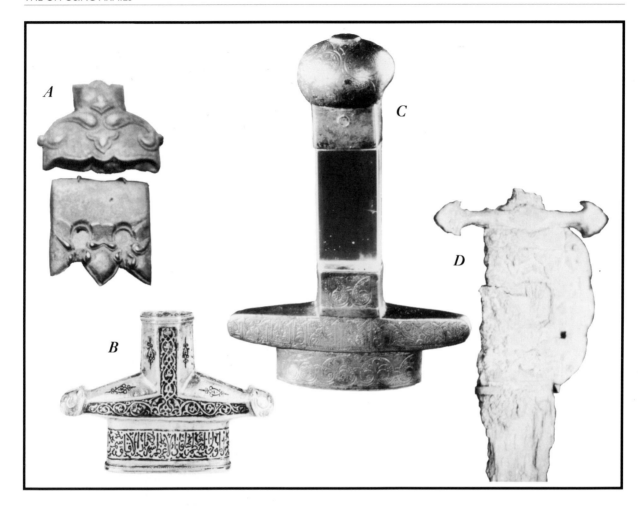

Saladin inherited. In addition to sword making in Damascus, Mosul had an arms market as did neighbouring Baghdad.

Saladin was criticized for seizing horses and weaponry from Nur al Din's arsenals when the latter died, yet it was clearly important for an ambitious ruler to get his hands on as much scarce military *matériel* as possible. The value of such equipment made the capture of enemy stores worth recording and when a Latin garrison surrendered it invariably had to leave its arms behind. The Muslims could also demand tribute in weapons even including horse armours from the Latin States, while in January 1188 a Byzantine embassy, as a mark of friendship, gave Saladin 400 mail hauberks, 4,000 lances and 5,000 swords captured from an Italo-Norman army. Swords were also imported commercially from both Byzantium and Europe — the latter in direct contravention of a Papal ban. But an extended

▲ *A: 12th- to 14th-century bronze matrices from Iran for shaping sword guards and scabbard lockets (Metropolitan Museum, New York, inv. 1980.210,103); B: 13th to 14th-century gold sword quillons from Iran (City Art Museum, St. Louis); C: 10th-century*

bronze quillons and pommel from Egypt, decorated with Sura CXII of the Koran (ex-Storm Rice Collection); D: 10th-century sabre with bronze quillons and scabbard mounts, from Iran (Metropolitan Museum, New York, inv. 40.170.168).

campaign could pose huge problems of supply.

The weapons used in Saladin's armies included spears, swords, maces, axes, javelins, composite bows, crossbows and occasionally lassos; the main protection being shields, lamellar cuirasses, mail hauberks including the padded cloth-covered *kazaghand*, and helmets. The popular image of lightly armed Saracens wielding equally light sabres is far from reality. Many if not most Islamic swords were still straight though the curved sabre, long known in Turkish Central Asia, had appeared in Persia by the 9th or 10th centuries. The composite bow had long been the main missile weapon of the Middle East but one notable change during the Crusading era was from the angled, so-called 'Hun' bow to the smoothly recurved 'Turkish' type. The earlier form would have given an easy initial draw followed by a smooth increase in tension but suffered from wasted energy with the release of the massive non-flexing 'ears'. The long ears could also be a problem for a horse-archer whereas the new smoothly recurved bow was shorter, less likely to hit the rider's own horse and had more efficient energy transfer to its arrow. On the other hand this so-called Turkish type had a stiffer draw and might be less accurate in the hands of any but an expert archer. Sources indicating the ineffect-iveness of Islamic archery against Crusader armour are widely misunderstood, referring as they do to long-range harassment intended to injure unprotected horses rather than to kill men. Tests have, in fact, shown that mail offered little resistance to arrows, even those shot with the inferior longbows used in western Europe. On the other hand the shock-absorbing lamellar armours of the Turks would almost certainly have given greater protection.

The Size of Saladin's Army

Even today it is widely assumed that Islamic armies were huge and that the valiant Crusaders were overwhelmed by numbers. This is not born out by the facts. Of course the manpower potential of the Muslim states was far greater than that of the Latin States in Syria and Palestine, but, as in Europe, only a small proportion normally took part in warfare. Nevertheless large auxiliary forces could be mustered — for a short while — around a ruler's professional *askar*. Egypt could afford quite large armies, though even under the Fatimids these were nowhere near as big as sometimes believed, reaching a maximum of 25,000 at best. In his early days as Nur al Din's governor in Egypt, Saladin inherited some Fatimid regiments and records show that in 1169

▼ *Nobleman. The weaponry of the high aristocracy was highly decorated, this man's helmet being partially gilded and his coif covered in rich material. The feet of his mail* chausses *are covered in iron scales, a very advanced feature for this period. Illustration by Angus Mc Bride.*

'Fight between Roland and Faragut': relief carvings of c. ad 1138 on the façade of the Church of San Zeno in Verona. The ideal of knightly combat began with the 'breaking of lances' and concluded with swords, as it did in the Islamic heroic tales of the Arab Middle East. (Author's photographs)

he had 8,640 regulars, excluding naval troops, of whom the most reliable were his own family's 500-strong following plus 3,000 Turcomans. At another review held on 11 September 1171 Saladin mustered 174 *tulb* cavalry squadrons (about 14,000 cavalry) while a further 20 squadrons were on duty elsewhere, plus some 7,000 Arab bedouin auxiliaries. A pro-Fatimid coup attempt in 1174 led to most of the old Fatimid units being disbanded and bedouin

auxiliaries were reduced to about 1,300. A further *ard* (review) held in 1181 listed Saladin's forces at 6,976 *tawashi* cavalry plus 1,553 *qaraghulam mamluks*. To this could be added the forces maintained by the governors of Syrian cities, though not all would be committed to one campaign at one time. Damascus is estimated to have had a garrison of about 1,000, Hims 500, Hama and its dependent towns 1,000 and Aleppo 1,000. The Jazira region could field a further

▶ *Two carved capitals in the cloisters of Monreale Cathedral, Sicily made in the late 12th century. The many carvings at Monreale show a greater variety of arms and armour than do the carvings of northern Europe and may reflect both climate and a specifically Mediterranean military tradition shared with Byzantium, the Arab countries and the Latin States of the Middle East. (Author's photographs)*

2,000 to 4,000 men including Mosul's own garrison which numbered 1,500 in the early 12th century.

The Crusader Forces

Most leading families of the Latin States rose from relatively humble origins, having made their fortunes early in the 12th century. Even so there were never enough trained warriors to defend the new territories and qualifications for knighthood were lowered so that pilgrims would settle. Even indigenous Christians where sometimes knighted in 12th-century Jerusalem. This, and the many marriages between Crusader warriors and local Christian women, led to a certain 'orientalization' of the Latin aristocracy. Yet this was very superficial and many of the supposed 'eastern fashions' were Byzantine rather than Middle Eastern. An influx of bourgeois Italian merchants

◀ Ghulam *cavalryman. Beneath his armour this élite horseman's costume is basically Turco-Iranian. His painted helmet has a gilded leather neck-guard and his lamellar cuirass is quite light. He is armed with an animal-headed mace, a curved sabre and has a heavy straight sword tucked beneath his saddle. Illustration by Rob Chapman.*

▶ *The mid to late 12th-century wall paintings at Cressac in central France, illustrating Templar knights fighting Nur al Din's army are well-known. Less famous are a series of cavalrymen along the lower register, shown here. The style of art is quite different and may reflect Spanish or even Middle Eastern influences brought back by Templars who had fought the Muslims. (Author's photograph)*

▶ *Early 13th-century carved capital showing a knight's destrier or war horse, in the cloisters of St-Trophime, Arles. (Author's photograph)*

was meanwhile seen as a social threat by the new aristocracy of Jerusalem. Knights claiming French origin also looked down on knights of Italian blood, and all were despised as half-breeds by men newly come from Europe.

The *Marechal* of each Latin State was in charge of recruitment, but his powers were limited by customary law. Knights, for example, were excused service on foot or where their horses could not carry them. Nevertheless men from knightly families would be involved in warfare from the age of fifteen and remained liable for military summons until sixty. On the other hand

service was not due if a knight lost his fief to the enemy. The frequent mention of *sodees* ('soldiers') did not always refer to paid mercenaries as in Europe. Instead many Latin *sodees* had fiefs of money or rent rather than land. Troops would also be drawn from other organizations owing feudal obligations such as the Church, towns, indigenous Christian landholders and the Military Orders. These would supply knights and mounted serjeants, plus large numbers of infantry. In emergencies an *arriere ban* would be declared in which, again theoretically, all free men had to muster. Infantry could also be recruited from

◄ 'Pharaoh's Army in the Red Sea', on a late 12th-century carved font in the church of San Frediano, Lucca. Both horsemen wear mail hauberks while the leading rider also has mail chausses covering his legs. (Author's photograph)

▶ 'Devils and Sinners' carved on the façade of the church of Ste-Foy, Conques, ad 1120-30. On the left a fully mailed knight, probably representing the sins of war or pride, is tipped on to his head. On the right devils are armed with 'demonic' weapons including a pick, a ball-and-chain and a crossbow. (Author's photographs)

visiting pilgrims, of whom there were many in the Kingdom of Jerusalem. As such sources still remained inadequate the Latin States increasingly relied on mercenaries and the majority of mounted serjeants were probably hired outside the Middle East. Western mercenaries often stayed in almost permanent service though their contracts may have been renewed monthly. Penalties for deserting before a contract expired were, however, severe; a knight forfeiting his armour and other equipment, a common soldier having his hands pierced with a hot iron.

The Military Orders of Templars and Hospit-

allers tended to reflect the aggressive attitudes of the newcomers, rather than the more cautious Latin settlers, and their motivation had much in common with the *muttawiyah* religious volunteers of the Muslim side. Among indigenous and non-feudal troops, the *Turcopoles* were by far the most important. The concept and the name were copied from the Byzantines but also had something in common with the Muslim system of slave-recruited *mamluks*, most being converted Muslim prisoners of war. No Muslim soldiers could be found in Latin service, though the Latin States did employ Muslim clerks. Nor were Jews

enlisted as they were regarded as sympathetic to the Muslim side. Siege engineers were recruited from various indigenous Christian communities and here Armenians took a leading role. In fact Armenians proved to be the most sympathetic of eastern Christian sects, but were mostly found in the north, in the Principality of Antioch where they provided the bulk of the infantry. Maronites from what is now Lebanon furnished the Kingdom of Jerusalem with infantry archers but were not fully integrated into the new feudal structure. Except for the largely pro-Muslim Nestorians, most of whom lived beyond Latin

territory in what is now Iraq and Iran, Syrian Orthodox or Jacobite Christians were regarded as the least reliable yet even they were needed as guides.

Organization of the Crusader Forces

As in feudal France, which the Latins of Syria took as their model, the King of Jerusalem commanded the army. His authority might be expected to have been great because the Latin States were highly militarized and the army of Jerusalem was a permanent structure due to the almost constant state of war. Failure to expand much beyond the coastal strip and failure to conquer any of the inland cities except Jerusalem meant that the Kingdom had to maintain an abnormally large defensive army — but it also meant that it lacked land to support such an army by normal feudal means. Theoretically the King could demand that his knights serve a full year, much longer than was seen in the West, but in reality the period was negotiated at the *Haute Cour* (High Court) as each campaign was planned. Even when war broke out the King was only first among equals, and divided authority led to difficulties when facing a disciplined foe. The Kingdom of Jerusalem was also financially weak, which caused great problems for an army relying so strongly on mercenaries.

By the late 12th century most Latin knights, even those who had land fiefs, lived in the towns like their *iqta*-holding Muslim counterparts. Money fiefs had been known since at least the 1130s, their holders receiving rents from ports, markets, tolls, commercial or industrial properties. In return they, like any feudal fief-holder, had specified military obligations such as maintaining a certain number of fully equipped knights or serjeants. In addition to knightly fiefs there were also serjeantry fiefs, some of which supported *Turcopoles*.

The command structure of the army of Jerusalem stuck closer to the established European system. The three great military officers of state were the *Senechal*, the *Connetable* and the *Marechal*. The *Senechal* was responsible for all fortifications except the King's own palace, for

◀ 'Guards of the High Priest' on a carved stone candlestick of c.1170, in the basilica of San Paolo fuori la Mura, Rome. Two wear fluted conical helmets, one clearly secured by a chin-strap, while the kneeling soldier may have a quilted gambeson beneath his mail hauberk. (Author's photograph)

▼ Below left: these two men fighting on foot lack body armour. Late 12th-century carved capital in the cloisters of Monreale Cathedral, Sicily. (Author's photograph)

▼ Below right: another carved capital in the Monreale cloisters shows an archer with a quiver at his belt. (Author's photograph)

▶ Infantry are also shown in this small mid 12th-century relief carving of 'The Betrayal' in the crypt of Pistoia Cathedral. The men lack body armour but have helmets, spears and long shields which can cover them from chin to feet. (Author's photograph)

▲ *This pair of confronted archers on an 11th- to 12th-century carved altar in the church of Santa Maria in Valle Porclaneta, southern Italy, both have the old form of angled composite bow. (Author's photographs)*

garrisons and provisions. On campaign the *Senechal* usually led the King's own *bataille* or division under the King's direct command. The *Connetable* commanded the army except when the King was present. He also organized the muster, sorted out various *bataille* divisions in battle or on the march, gave them their duties and checked the readiness of knights, serjeants and squires. The knights were in fact the *Connetable*'s particular responsibility. The *Marechal*, of whom there might be more than one, was second in command to the *Connetable*. He was directly in charge of recruitment, particularly of mercenaries, controlling their pay and equipment as well as organizing other military *matériel*, horses and baggage animals for the army. The *Grand Turcopolier* commanded the King's *Turcopoles* and was under the immediate command of the *Marechal*, the only other *Turcopoles* being those of the Military Orders.

A knight often led four or five mounted serjeants, but in general serjeants seem to have formed a military reserve, not normally summoned to the first muster. The numbers of fighting troops expected from different fiefs varied considerably, great baronies like that of Jaffa or Galilee supporting 100 knights while a small fief like that of 'the wife of Gobert Vernier' supported only one. The numbers of serjeants also varied; 500 being maintained by the Patriarch of Jerusalem, 25 by the fief of Le Herin (Yarin), as did the numbers of mercenaries, ranging from 500 from the Patriarch of Jerusalem to 25 from Le Herin.

Heraldry may have been more advanced in the Latin States than in many parts of Europe. The Kingdom of Jerusalem certainly had its own great banner in the late 12th century, the Arab chronicler Baha al Din describing it as being '...on a staff as tall as a minaret and set up on a cart drawn by mules. It had a white background with red spots. The top of the staff was surmounted by a cross.' In other words it was a *carroccio* like those used as rallying points by the armies of medieval Italian cities. There is, however, no evidence for any form of permanent navy in the Kingdom of Jerusalem during the 12th century, though the coastal cities did have their own local shipping.

Crusader Tactics

There clearly was a 'Science of War' in 12th-century Europe, spanning broad strategic thinking to the employment of specialized troops. Large-scale set-piece battles were, however, rare simply because they were unpredictable and very risky. So, in addition to sieges, Western warfare revolved around raids and skirmishing in which there was plenty of scope for tactical skill. When a large battle did take place it hardly ever depended on cavalry alone, despite the dominant position of the knight. These traditions of warfare were transplanted to the Latin States in Syria and Palestine where there were few changes during the 12th century. The role of infantry in support of cavalry remained the same while the latter may even have lagged behind their European cousins when it came to adopting new tactics such as the couched lance.

How far the armies of the Latin States were influenced by their neighbours remains unclear. Even the knights were essentially part-time warriors and this may have limited their ability to learn from professional Byzantine soldiers, while cultural factors made it difficult for the Latins to copy their Muslim foes. Many Latin knights had experience of fighting within — as well as against — Muslim armies because it was common for men of the Latin States to serve as mercenaries under the Saljuq Sultans of Anatolia. Events prove that the Latins did evolve effective tactics against the Muslims. These, however, were essentially defensive and were designed to ensure the survival of the Latin States, not the total destruction of its foes. Major battles were avoided in the knowledge that if the field army were seriously weakened the towns and castles of the Kingdom would be vulnerable; particularly as the mustering of a large army meant reducing garrisons to a bare minimum. Obtaining enough remounts was another perennial problem for the Latin armies. In the Western tradition of knightly warfare it was considered bad form, as well as financially stupid, to kill or injure an enemy's horse. The Muslim armies, however, made a point of attacking the Crusaders' horses with spears and arrows.

Weather had a major impact on warfare in the Middle East. As a result summonses to muster were usually issued in early spring. Troops, pack animals and any additional livestock would be assembled. The army would then remain in camp to watch an invading enemy or be arranged into an order of march known by the originally Arabic name of *caravan*. According to the Old French Rule of the Templars, knights would assemble ahead of their squires, but the squires would be sent ahead with the knights' lances, shields and warhorses (which were only to be ridden in battle) during the actual march. The need to maintain cohesion on the march was fully understood, as was the vital role of infantry in protecting the knights' horses from enemy harassment. In open country such armies marched in a box-like formation with infantry surrounding the cavalry. In broken or mountainous terrain an army generally marched in columns.

Regulations for making camp are again best seen in the Templars' Old French Rule. This has brother knights setting up their tents around a tented chapel. In secular armies the commander's tent would presumably have been at the centre. Squires would then be sent to forage for firewood and water, though none might go beyond earshot of the camp's bell. If the alarm were sounded those nearest the trouble would rush to repel the enemy while others gathered at the chapel-tent to await orders. In a secular camp one could imagine the knights gathering at the commander's tent. Raiding and reconnaissance operations were given the French name of *chevaucher*. Here knights carried their own armour behind their saddles. Infantry would sometimes also be carried on the horses' cruppers. *Turcopoles* played a leading role on such expeditions and reconnaissance was the only time when the *Turcopolier* could command knights.

If the Latin army did commit itself to a set-piece battle, infantry were drawn up in front of the cavalry, the latter charging through gaps in the foot soldiers' ranks. The role of the infantry was to protect the cavalry's horses, rather than the riders, yet the infantry remained essential if a knightly charge was to be effective. On the other hand the Latins' reliance on infantry made their

▲ *Combat between galleys and a two-masted merchant ship on a late 13th-century painted beam from Catalonia. Both galleys have their beaks or rams supported by rope or chain, exactly as shown in a 5th-century late Roman manuscript. (Art Museum of Barcelona)*

armies slow and unmanoeuvrable compared to their Muslim foes. The structure and size of cavalry *eschielles* or squadrons varied but in general it seems that, in the Middle East, horsemen were split into smaller units than in Europe in an attempt to deal with fast and tactically flexible foes. Such small groups, however, were always in danger of being surrounded and engaged to exhaustion even if protected from mortal wounds by their heavy armour.

Although the knightly charge remained the Latin armies' only real offensive tactic it was effective if used properly, but, because it was a response to the enemy's actions, a charge could rarely be planned beforehand and it also left the initiative with the enemy. As the Muslims developed counter-measures so the effectiveness of the Latin charge declined. Lighter Muslim horsemen were in any case generally able to get out of the way by opening and closing their own ranks or wheeling aside. When such manoeuvres were not possible the Muslims could feign flight, whereupon the knights often lost their cohesion if they attempted to pursue. Even Muslim infantry, once they had learned the bitter lessons of the early 12th century, generally seem to have been able to escape such charges.

In contrast with this information about the cavalry, almost nothing is known of the organization of infantry in open battle, though more is known about siege warfare. Most Crusader castles were not sited on the frontiers, but, occupying the same sites as previous Byzantine and Islamic fortifications, were scattered about. These castles, often built at great speed, had varied designs depending on their situation. Throughout the 12th century most were simple and even primitive, the great Crusader castles which now dot the region either dating from the 13th century or having been extensively rebuilt by Muslim architects after their recapture. Not until the 13th century, when the Latins finally accepted that they had been forced on to the defensive, were fortifications provisioned to withstand a long siege. Each would have been commanded by a *chatelain*. Town garrisons would include knights and serjeants who manned both walls and gates, while the untrained burgesses were only entrusted with defending the walls, using crossbows and javelins.

Weaponry of the Crusader Forces

The Latin States were never famous centres of weapons manufacture though some burgesses of Jerusalem were listed as shield-makers. By far the bulk of their military equipment was imported from Europe and probably came from Italy or via Italian merchants. Captured Islamic weapons were also reused and the Order of Templars had special rules concerning these. Otherwise the weapons used in the Latin States were the same as those of western Europe. Radulfus Niger, writing allegorically in the very year of Hattin on how the Kingdom of Jerusalem should be supported, listed these as spurs, *chausses* (iron leggings), hauberks, *cuirie* (leather cuirass), helmets with face

49

protection, swords, horses, shields, lances, horse-harness, horse-armour, infantry weapons, flags and banners, and a variety of siege machines. How far the mid 13th-century Rule of the Temple reflected the 12th-century situation is unclear, but it stated that a brother knight should have mail hauberk and *chausses*, a light brimmed *chapel de fer* helmet, mail *coif*, possibly an arming cap, an *espaliere* shoulder-piece (perhaps of mail or padded), a quilted jupon or *gambeson*, a sword, lance, *masse turque* (Turkish form of mace), shield and couteau d'arme (large dagger plus two smaller knifes for non-military uses). His horse would have a *caparison* (covering cloth) and the knight should also keep a leather sack for his mail hauberk. Serjeants, again in the Rule of the Templars, had a smaller mail *haubergeon* which lacked mittens for the hands, and their mail *chausses* should lack feet to that they could walk in comfort.

Specific information about infantry equipment is rare but the *chansons de geste* poems of the period constantly refer to the foot soldiers' mail hauberks, long-hafted *gisarme* axes, 'Danish' axes which probably had heavy bearded blades, maces, *faussars* which may have been early forms of single-edged *falchions*, pikes, javelins, bows and crossbows. The European knight's prejudice against archery has perhaps been exaggerated. None the less the adoption of the crossbow as a

▶ *Cavalry serjeant. This man's arms and armour suggests southern Italian or Siculo-Norman origins and is relatively light. He wears no coif beneath his tall conical helmet and no mittens over his hands. The decoration of his horse harness also betrays Islamic and Byzantine influence. Illustration by Angus McBride.*

weapon of war instead of merely a hunting weapon was seen as a social and a military threat. In 1139 the Pope's Lateran Council attempted to ban the use of the crossbow, and perhaps also the ordinary bow, in war except when used against 'infidels'. Early crossbows often seem to have been made of laburnum wood and they had a very long draw compared to later medieval versions. Bows of composite construction, giving much greater power-for-weight, were incorporated into crossbows late in the 12th century, but when this idea reached the Latin States is uncertain. A lack of direct influence from the Middle Eastern composite bow upon the European composite crossbow is suggested by the fact that the two

weapons are constructed in totally different ways.

Horse harness was a major concern for the knightly élite. In addition to a leather-covered, wood-framed saddle with its *afeutremens* (felt padding) and *arcons* (raised cantle), the knight's horse would have had a saddle-cloth, single or doubled girths, breeching and breast straps. The latter or *poitral* had to be very strong to take the shock of impact when a rider struck with his couched lance.

The siege machinery available to the Latin States was basically the same as that used by the Muslims. *Fondifles* were slings, probably of the staff-sling variety, while the main stone-throwing devices were *mangonels* and *perieres* or *petraria*.

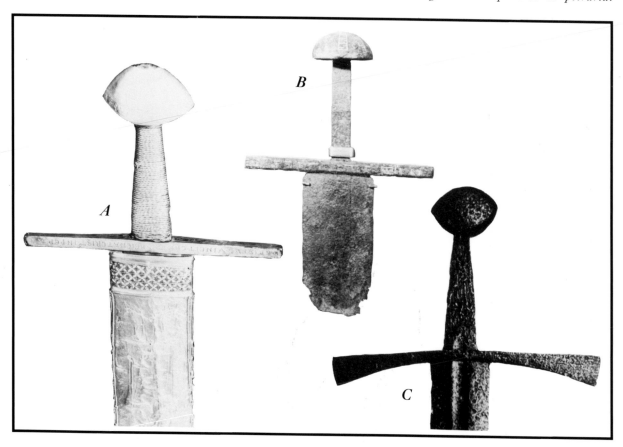

▲*Christian swords. A: Sword of St. Maurice, German, ad 1198-1215 (Kunsthistorische Museum, Vienna); B: 12th-century Spanish sword hilt (Museum Eserjito, Madrid); C:* *French c. 1157-75 (Royer Collection).*

The fully developed counterweight *trebuchet* was an astonishing machine. Recent experiments with a trebuchet having a 200-kilogram counterweight threw a 15-kilogram ball 180 metres, a 47-kilogram ball 100 metres, all within a target 6 metres square. The term *periere* or *petraria* was used more loosely but often referred to torsion

engines like the ancient Roman stone-throwing devices. The *petraria turquesa* (Turkish stone-machine) of about AD 1202 was clearly a torsion-powered device, probably similar to the twin-armed crossbow-like machine known in Islam as the *qaws ziyar*.

▲ Most of what can now be seen of the castle of Krak (Karak) dates from after it was retaken by the Muslims, as is the case with most of the larger so-called Crusader castles. But these outer walls and towers probably formed a military base for Reynald of Châtillon's expeditions against his neighbours. (Author's photograph)

The Size of the Crusader Army

Contrary to yet another widespread myth, the military élite or knightly class of the late 12th-century Kingdom of Jerusalem was neither enfeebled nor degenerate. The settlers had not gone soft, as their uncultured European contemporaries claimed, but had learned to take a realistic approach to warfare with their Muslim neighbours. Even the town-based knights of the Latin States clung to the ideas and aspirations of knightly chivalry, following the latest fashions from France and Italy.

Until the massive losses of territory which followed Hattin, the Kingdom of Jerusalem could field a substantial army. According to a register based on records from the reign of Baldwin IV, the total military establishment of the Kingdom numbered 675 knights and 5,025 serjeants plus *Turcopoles* and mercenaries. At best Jerusalem could muster up to 1,000 knights including contingents sent from the 200 knights maintained by the County of Tripoli and the 700 of the Principality of Antioch. At most times there would also be knights among visiting pilgrims from Europe.

Meanwhile the Templars maintained a highly disciplined regiment of up to 300 knights in the Latin States, plus several hundred serjeants and *Turcopoles*. In 1168 the Hospitallers had promised 500 knights and 500 *Turcopoles* for an invasion of Egypt, though whether they could really muster such a force remains unclear as there never seem to have been more than 300 brother knights in the Middle East at any one time. Local indigenous troops would also push up the size of the army.

OPPOSING PLANS

The Sultan had to make a major effort against the Latin States to maintain his prestige among fellow Muslims. Saladin's recovery from a serious illness may also have made him realize that death was not far off and that it was now or never. The first part of the year was taken up with raiding to test the enemy's strength and to weaken him. But once Saladin's main force was committed across the frontier there was no further raiding. All efforts were directed to enticing the Latin field army into a major battle. This also had to be done quickly for it was difficult for Saladin's army to remain in the field for a long time. The Sultan may also have taken into account the losses inflicted on the Military Orders at the Springs of Cresson earlier that year, since they were the most effective troops in the Latin army.

Skirmishing failed to lure the Latins out of their strong defensive position so Saladin committed his forces to a full-scale assault on Tiberius. In so doing he put himself in a very dangerous position with the possibility of being caught between two enemy forces, but the gamble worked and the Christians marched to relieve Tiberius. Everything depended on not allowing the Latins to reach adequate water supplies once they left Sephorie (Saffuriyah) and Saladin then staked everything on a major battle before the Latin field army came off the dry plateau to reach water at Lake Tiberius. The likely area of battle had, of course, already been reconnoitred by Saladin's scouts. His plan for the following day was simple. The enemy must still not reach water, his infantry must be separated from his cavalry and none must escape. In the event things turned out almost exactly as Saladin hoped, although more Latin troops did escape from the battle than is generally realized.

Events after Saladin's victory at Hattin were simply a case of taking full advantage of the destruction of the Latin field army by capturing as many fortified places as possible before another European Crusade arrived. Saladin's preoccupation with the threat from the West is shown by his seizure of the coastal towns first, before going on to take the greatest prize of all — the Holy City of Jerusalem.

Having assembled the largest army he could at the traditional mustering point of Sephorie, King Guy at first stuck to traditional policy when faced

▲ *The interior of Saffuriyah (Sephorie) castle in Galilee. The basic structure dates from the Crusader period. (Author's photograph)*

Campaigns of 1187

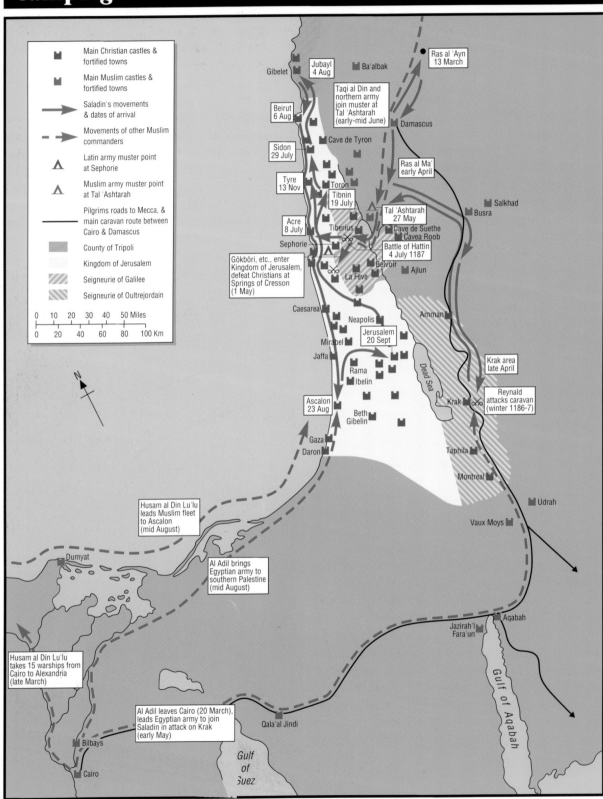

Main Christian castles & fortified towns

Main Muslim castles & fortified towns

Saladin's movements & dates of arrival

Movements of other Muslim commanders

Latin army muster point at Sephorie

Muslim army muster point at Tal 'Ashtarah

Pilgrims roads to Mecca, & main caravan route between Cairo & Damascus

County of Tripoli

Kingdom of Jerusalem

Seigneurie of Galilee

Seigneurie of Oultrejordain

0 10 20 30 40 50 Miles
0 20 40 60 80 100 Km

N

Ras al 'Ayn 13 March

Jubayl 4 Aug

Gibelet

Ba'albak

Taqi al Din and northern army join muster at Tal 'Ashtarah (early-mid June)

Beirut 6 Aug

Damascus

Cave de Tyron

Sidon 29 July

Ras al Ma' early April

Tyre 13 Nov

Toron

Tibnin 19 July

Salkhad

Busra

Tal 'Ashtarah 27 May

Acre 8 July

Tiberius

Cave de Suethe
Cavea Roob

Sephorie

Battle of Hattin 4 July 1187

Gökböri, etc., enter Kingdom of Jerusalem, defeat Christians at Springs of Cresson (1 May)

Belvoir

La Fève

Ajlun

Caesarea

Amman

Neapolis

Jerusalem 20 Sept

Mirabel

Jaffa

Rama

Ibelin

Krak area late April

Ascalon 23 Aug

Beth Gibelin

Dead Sea

Krak

Reynald attacks caravan (winter 1186-7)

Gaza

Daron

Husam al Din Lu'lu leads Muslim fleet to Ascalon (mid August)

Taphila

Montreal

Udrah

Vaux Moys

Al Adil brings Egyptian army to southern Palestine (mid August)

Dumyat

Husam al Din Lu'lu takes 15 warships from Cairo to Alexandria (late March)

Aqabah

Jazirah'l Fara'un

Al Adil leaves Cairo (20 March), leads Egyptian army to join Saladin in attack on Krak (early May)

Qala'al Jindi

Gulf of Suez

Bilbays

Cairo

Gulf of Aqabah

with an invasion from the direction of Damascus. The army stayed put in its strong situation and by threatening Saladin's more exposed positions, hoped that the Muslims would eventually retreat. It was a predictable reaction to a predictable attack. The fact that Guy then decided to relieve Tiberius and meet Saladin in battle has been described as unusual, yet such a reaction had been attempted before — successfully. Guy may have feared blame for the damage being caused by Saladin's troops, but he may also have hoped to catch and destroy the Muslim army west of Lake Tiberius, where its escape would be difficult.

Once Saladin had outmanoeuvred the Latins, however, the latter faced a battle seriously low on water but still within striking distance of the springs at Hattin village. Guy therefore marched in that direction with his infantry, as usual, protecting his cavalry. The only other course would have been an all-out attack on Saladin's main force. This suggestion was rejected, though the sources do not say why. Perhaps the Christian army's poor morale and raging thirst made a move away from water impossible.

Following the disaster at Hattin all that the remaining Latin garrisons could do was make the best terms they could or hang on until relief arrived. The latter was very long in coming but for the coastal cities there was always hope of help arriving by sea. This was why some garrisons fought so hard and why the efforts of Tyre (Sur) were eventually rewarded.

▶ *'Chedorlaomer defeated by Abraham', mid 13th-century painted ceiling in the Baptistry, Parma. Such scenes portray the ideal of European cavalry combat with lances, though here only the first knight on the left is using his lance in the approved couched manner.*

▶ *'Battle between the Banu Zabba and the Banu Shayba' in the late 12th—early 13th-century Warqa wa Gulshah manuscript from Azarbayjan. While the arrows fly thick and fast, most of the men are wielding swords. (Topkapi Library, Istanbul, Ms. Haz. 841)*

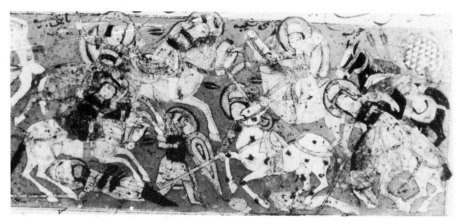

THE CAMPAIGN

Despite a truce between Saladin and the Kingdom of Jerusalem, the situation east of the River Jordan was volatile by the start of 1187, while farther south Reynald of Châtillon was still demanding tolls from Muslim caravans travelling between Egypt and Syria. Suddenly, that winter, Reynald attacked a large caravan, capturing the travellers and their escort. Perhaps he felt that such a large escort breached the truce, or that Saladin's support for Count Raymond in his quarrel with King Guy (see above) had already done so, or perhaps he was simply 'piratical' as some Muslim chroniclers believed. The story that one of Saladin's sisters and her son were with this caravan is untrue, but Reynald's actions, plus King Guy's inability to get the prisoners released, gave Saladin a perfect excuse to renew the war.

At the start of the Muslim year of 583 AH (13 March 1187) the Sultan led the troops in Damascus to the well-watered area of Ras al Mai' and sent letters to neighbouring countries asking for volunteers for a forthcoming *jihad*. A week later his bother Al Adil, the governor of Egypt, led his forces out of Cairo towards Syria. Meanwhile Husam al Din Lu'lu took fifteen galleys down the Nile to Alexandria. Far to the north Taqi al Din and his troops reached Aleppo, from where they watched the frontier with Antioch. It was now the Muslim month of Muharram when huge numbers of pilgrims would be travelling home from Mecca. So Saladin left the troops who were assembling at Ras al Mai' under the command of his son Al Afdal and, perhaps fearing another raid by Reynald of Châtillon, took his own guards south of Busra to keep watch on the Pilgrim road. On 20 April Taqi al Din moved forward to the fortress of Harenc (Harim), right on the frontier of Antioch and, at about the same time, Saladin's small force raided south into Oultrejordain. On 26 April, the day

that Al Adil's Egyptian army was expected to reach Aqabah, Saladin attacked Krak itself, confining the garrison so that Muslim irregulars could ravage the entire province. Saladin also ordered Al Afdal to raid neighbouring Latin territory but then countermanded these orders, telling Al Afdal to await further developments.

Meanwhile the leading barons of the Kingdom of Jerusalem assembled to persuade King Guy to seek a reconciliation with Count Raymond who was still holed up in his wife's town of Tiberius. A delegation was sent, including Balian d'Ibelin, the Master of the Hospitallers, the Archbishop of Tyre, Reynald of Sidon and Gerard de Ridefort, Master of the Temple. It left on 29 April, making its leisurely way towards Tiberius. But next day an envoy from Al Afdal arrived at Tiberius with a message from Saladin. This politely asked his 'friend' Count Raymond to allow a Muslim reconnaissance party across his land the following day. They wished, the letter said, no harm to Raymond's lordship of Galilee, but wanted to reach King Guy's Royal Domain around Acre. Not knowing of the approaching delegation Raymond agreed on condition that the Muslims returned the same the day and inflicted no damage.

On the morning of 1 May the Muslim party passed beneath Tiberius' walls and turned west. It was commanded by Muzaffar al Din Gökböri with his troops from the Jazira, and other Turkish *amir*s including Qaymaz al Najmi with a squadron from Damascus and Dildirim al Yaruqi with men from Aleppo. Al Afdal himself seems to have remained with a larger force at Al Qahwani south-east of Lake Tiberius. Count Raymond now learned of King Guy's approaching delegation from Jerusalem and sent them a warning. By that time the delegation no longer included Reynald of Sidon or Balian d'Ibelin who had agreed to catch the others up at La Feve (Al Fulah). The main part of the delegation had also heard about the planned Muslim reconnaissance the previous night, through Raymond's warnings to his own troops in Galilee. Gerard de Ridefort summoned all Templar troops in the area and at nightfall on 30 April the Marshal of the Temple brought 90 knights from the castle at Caco (Al Qaqun). Next morning Gerard led these and his own followers to Nazareth where they were joined by secular knights before riding east towards the Springs of Cresson (Ayn Juzah) near the present village of Ayn Mahil. By this time Gerard had a force of about 130 knights, an unknown number of *Turcopoles* and up to 400 infantry. Gökböri's force was said to consist of 7,000 men though this is a huge exaggeration, 700 seeming more likely.

The course of the battle which followed is clear, even if the numbers are not. Against the advice of the Master of the Hospital and the Marshal of the Temple, Gerard insisted on a sudden charge against the Muslims. This has been presented as a case of suicidal overconfidence, yet the Muslim chroniclers indicate that the brief struggle was a close-run thing fought out in a forest. The Templars, Hospitallers and other cavalry caught their enemy unawares, though in so doing they left their infantry behind. Dildirim al Yaruqi's troops from Aleppo received the brunt of the charge and were praised for standing firm. It seems that Gökböri and Qaymaz al Najmi then led a counter-charge with spear and sword, the Latin cavalry being surrounded and overwhelmed. Only Gerard de Ridefort and a handful of knights escaped death or capture, the Muslims then scattering the Christian infantry before pillaging the surrounding area. The fact that Gökböri's force next returned across Raymond's lands without doing further damage says a lot for their discipline.

This rout at the Springs of Cresson on 1 May 1187 had a greater impact than might be realized. Although it encouraged King Guy and Count Raymond to patch up their quarrel, the Hospitallers had lost their chief and the Templars had suffered severe losses. Latin morale may not have been affected but that of the Muslims certainly increased. At about the same time a fleet from the Byzantine Emperor Isaac raided Cyprus which was being held by a rival claimant to the imperial throne. Unfortunately this rebel was an ally of the Latin Principality of Antioch and as a result Isaac Angelus was accused of siding with Saladin. Relations between Latin and Greek Orthodox Christians thus sunk to a new low on the eve of Saladin's final assault.

The Armies Muster

To the south Al Adil's army had joined Saladin's own small force to ravage Oultrejordain and encourage local peasantry to migrate into Muslim-ruled areas. By late May all that Reynald was holding were the castles of Krak and Montreal. Nevertheless Gökböri's victory at the Springs of Cresson may have undermined Saladin's strategy as it was now clear that the enemy was moving to meet a threat from Damascus rather than coming to rescue Oultrejordain. So Saladin returned north with some of the Egyptian troops while Al Adil returned to Cairo. He also told Al Afdal to check

▲ *Jabal Tabur (Mount Tabor) rising above the other hills of Galilee, seen from the Arab village of Ayn Mahil, close to the Springs of Cresson where Gökböri and his men utterly defeated Gerard de Ridefort's Templars who attacked them on 1 May 1187. (Author's photograph)*

the condition of pasture and water-supplies for he needed a mustering point for a large army. In the end Nur al Din's camping ground at Tal 'Ashtarah was selected. There Saladin and Al Afdal joined forces on 27 May. Urgent messages were sent throughout Syria and the Jazira for troops to join them. So far Taqi al Din's role had been to inhibit military action by the Principality of Antioch or the Armenians of Cilicia, but at the beginning of June he made a truce with Antioch and led the bulk of his troops south to join Saladin. Soon there were troops from all over Syria, Mardin, Nisibin, Diyarbakr and neighbouring regions of what is now south-eastern Turkey, plus Mosul and Irbil in northern Iraq, encamped around Tal 'Ashtarah. On 24 June a great *ard* or review was held at Tasil a few miles away, and the army was found to number some 12,000 professional cavalry plus a large number of less effective troops; a total of about 45,000.

◀ *The small Crusader castle at Saffuriyah (Sephorie) with its elaborately carved doorway. The upper part of the building was reconstructed by the local Arab leader Tahar al Umar in 1745. In June 1187 the Latin army mustered at the nearby springs. (Author's photograph)*

◀ *The springs at Muzayrib in early spring. The fertile plain north of the Yarmuk valley has many such springs which served as muster points for Muslim armies before campaigns against the Crusaders. Here there would be not only water for men and animals but also grass for the horses. (Author's photograph)*

Events were also moving in the Kingdom of Jerusalem. After the disaster at the Springs of Cresson Count Raymond sent home the troops Saladin had sent to strengthen Tiberius, then publicly did homage to Guy as King. Yet great bitterness remained beneath the surface, particularly between Raymond and Gerard de Ridefort, Master of the Templars. Latin losses at Cresson may have included 130 knights while Saladin's ravaging of Oultrejordain also weakened

its potential. Faced with such a serious situation King Guy sent out the *arriere ban* at the end of May, summoning all able-bodied free Christian men. Meanwhile Gerard de Ridefort handed over money given by King Henry II and with this the King recruited mercenaries, mostly mounted serjeants, who now displayed the arms of the King of England. His army mustered at springs just south of the castle of Sephorie (Saffuriyah). By the end of June it totalled some 1,200 knights, up

Left: Arab cavalryman.
Right: Serjeant with banner.
Illustration by Angus McBride.

◄ *The falls at Al Hamah near the western end of the Yarmuk gorge. Such abundant water sources are rare in this part of the Middle East and both sides sought to control them. These falls lay within the Terre de Suethe, which formed an eastern extension of the Latin seigniory of Galilee. (Author's photograph)*

◄ *Centre, the Bab al Tumm where the River Jordan flows out of Lake Tiberius. Saladin's army crossed into Palestine by the bridge of Sannabrah to the left of this picture, either on 30 June or 2 July. (Author's photograph)*

▼ *Bottom, an Israeli settlement now lies next to the site of the Palestinian village of Kafr Sabt, destroyed after being conquered by the Israelis in 1948. Here Saladin set up his main camp at the beginning of June. (Author's photograph)*

▶ *Remains of the Crusader church and city walls at the north-eastern corner of medieval Tiberius which lay south of modern Tiberius. The Sultan's main position was beyond the edge of the plateau in the distance. (Author's photograph)*

to 4,000 lighter cavalry serjeants and *Turcopoles*. Its 15,000 to 18,000 infantry would have been of mixed value, ranging from professional crossbowmen to inexperienced locals. This gave Saladin a numerical advantage of three to two though the Muslims were inferior in armoured cavalry. Christian leaders included the Masters of the Temple and the Hospital, the Count of Tripoli, Reynald de Châtillon, Balian d'Ibelin, Reginald of Sidon, and Walter Garnier, the Lord of Caesarea.

During Saladin's review of his army the basic array had been agreed. Taqi al Din commanded the right, Gökböri the left, Saladin the centre which may also have included van and rearguards. On 26 June they set out on the first stage of their march and made camp at Khisfin on the Golan Heights. The following day the army wound down the southern tip of the Heights to encamp at Al Qahwani, a marshy area between Lake Tiberius and the Rivers Jordan and Yarmouk. Small parties were now sent across the Jordan to ravage a wide area between Nazareth, Tiberius and Mount Tabor — the invasion had begun.

King Guy was holding a Council of leaders in Acre but moved up to Sephorie on hearing the news. Precisely when Saladin's main force crossed the Jordan is not clear, but it is likely to have been on 30 June. Tiberius was blockaded while scouts went towards Sephorie and the bulk of the army camped at Cafarsset (Kafr Sabt). Here there were several springs midway between Tiberius and the enemy's main position. On 1 July Saladin himself approached Sephorie, perhaps hoping to lure King Guy out. That same day the Sultan made a reconnaissance of Lubia (Lubiyah) which lay on an alternative route between Sephorie and Tiberius.

On the 2nd Saladin attacked Tiberius with part of his army, including the siege engineers and their cumbersome equipment, thus placing them between the Tiberius garrison and the main Christian army if the latter moved from Sephorie. With the lake on one side and steep hillsides on the other, escape would have been difficult in case of defeat and to guard against this Saladin remained at Cafarsset with most of the cavalry. Fortunately the Tiberius garrison had been reduced to an absolute minimum and the town fell by nightfall. The defenders and Count Raymond's gallant wife Countess Eschiva retreated to the citadel from where they continued to defy the Sultan's army.

Meanwhile King Guy held another Council at Sephorie. Count Raymond argued against marching to raise the siege of Tiberius because this was clearly what Saladin wanted. If they stayed put, however, Saladin would either have to retreat or attack the Christian army in a strong position. If the army marched east in high summer it would suffer acute thirst on a road that lacked adequate water sources and crossed a 'desert', by which Raymond probably meant that they would find no fodder for their horses. Many of the men at the Council still suspected Raymond of being a traitor because of his previous alliance with Saladin, and Gerard de Ridefort also accused him of cowardice. Yet for now Count Raymond's reasoning won the day and the army stayed put. During the night of 2/3 July, however, Gerard de Ridefort continued to badger King Guy with political as well as military arguments. Perhaps he also pointed out that King Henry of England's money had been spent — without consulting Henry — and that it should not now be wasted.

The Christian army awoke before sunrise on 3 July to hear that they were marching towards Tiberius after all. A variety of routes were available. They could swing south via Casal Robert (Kafr Kana) then north-east to join the main road to Tiberius near Touraan (Tur'an) which had a small spring, or they could head directly for Touraan by marching north and then east. A few kilometres east of Touraan the road divided, the main branch continuing via Saladin's main position at Cafarsset while another, also leading to Tiberius, ran in a northerly sweep via Lubia and the Horns of Hattin. About two kilometres from Tiberius both roads plunged down steep slopes to the Lake. The northern road between Touraan and Tiberius itself divided about two kilometres west of Lubia. From here a track went in an even more northerly sweep around the other side of the Horns of Hattin, down a steep slope to Hattin with its abundant spring and the even more spectacular Wadi Hammam gorge to the lake at Magdala (Al Majdal).

King Guy chose to go via Casal Robert. The army probably broke camp at about sunrise, then marched in three divisions with Count Raymond commanding the vanguard. King Guy led the centre where Christendom's greatest relic, the Holy Cross on which Christ was believed to have been crucified, was guarded by the bishops of Acre and Lidde (Lydda). Balian d'Ibelin commanded the rearguard where the Templars were also stationed. Each division would have consisted of cavalry protected on all sides by infantry. Portents and signs were already eroding the army's morale, which was perhaps never high as any local soldier knew that they were in for a long, hot, dusty and very thirsty march even if the enemy left them alone. As the march began, a half-crazed Muslim woman was thought to have laid a curse upon the army. A fire in which the nervous soldiers tried to burn the unfortunate lady supposedly left her unscathed and so a soldier split her head with an axe. The horses were said to have refused to drink before setting out — a very serious matter given the lack of water on the way.

When Saladin, outside Tiberius, heard that the enemy was on the march he immediately led his guards back to the main camp at Cafarsset, leaving a small force to watch Tiberius. Detachments were then sent to harass the Christian army but Saladin's main force does not appear to have made contact until King Guy reached Touraan at about 10 o'clock in the morning. Some Christians on the left flank may have drunk at Touraan's spring but the bulk of the army pressed on. Being denied a drink further eroded their morale. Harassment intensified as the Christians moved across Saladin's front, closer to his base at Cafarsset, with heat, thirst, dust, throbbing Muslim drums and now a steady wastage of horses struck down by arrows. At noon repeated attacks slowed the Christians' pace to a crawl and soon Count Raymond in the vanguard, which had reached the road junction near Manescalcia (Miskinah), was told that the rearguard had been forced to halt. At this point there was a major change of plan. Believing that the army could no longer fight its way across Saladin's front, Count Raymond convinced King Guy that they should swing left down a track to the springs at Hattin only six kilometres away. From there they could reach Lake Tiberius the next day.

The army was now probably spread over at least two kilometres on a relatively level plain, with Jabal Tur'an stretching along its left flank in

The March to Hattin

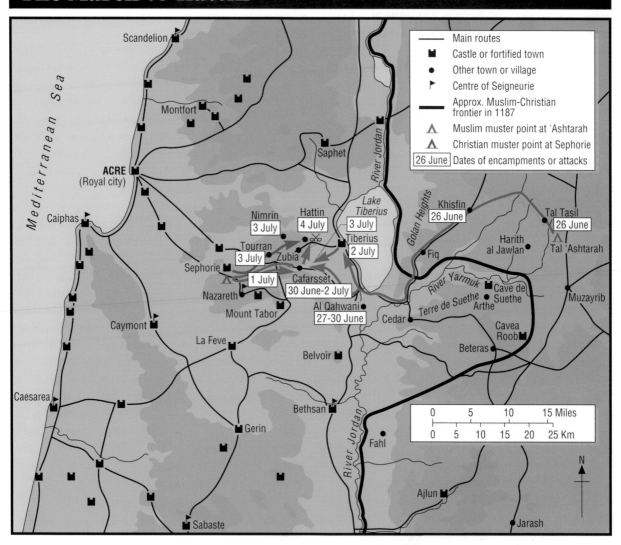

Map legend:
- Main routes
- ▉ Castle or fortified town
- ● Other town or village
- ▶ Centre of Seigneurie
- Approx. Muslim-Christian frontier in 1187
- ᴧ Muslim muster point at 'Ashtarah
- ᴧ Christian muster point at Sephorie
- 26 June Dates of encampments or attacks

Mediterranean Sea

Scandelion

Montfort

Saphet

River Jordan

ACRE (Royal city)

Caiphas

Nimrin
3 July

Hattin
4 July

Lake Tiberius
3 July

Tiberius
2 July

Golan Heights

Khisfin
26 June

Tal Tasil
26 June

Tourran
3 July

Zubia

Harith al Jawlan

Tal 'Ashtarah

Sephorie

Fiq

1 July

Cafarsset
30 June-2 July

River Yarmuk

Cave de Suethe

Muzayrib

Nazareth

Terre de Suethe

Arthe

Mount Tabor

Al Qahwani
27-30 June

Cedar

Cavea Roob

Caymont

Beteras

La Feve

Belvoir

Caesarea

Gerin

Bethsan

Fahl

River Jordan

Ajlun

Jarash

Sabaste

0   5   10   15 Miles
0   5   10   15   20   25 Km

N

▶ Tur'an is one of the few Arab villages to have survived the Israeli conquest. It lies at the foot of the Jabal Tur'an hill and has the only large spring between Saffuriyah and Hattin. King Guy's army passed by on 3 July but did not stop for water. (Author's photograph)

a series of wooded slopes ending in a small hill topped by the village of Nimrin. On its right flank, the villages of Sejera (Shajarah) and Lubia stood on other wooded hills. Ahead rose the Horns of Hattin with the waters of Lake Tiberius just visible to their right. Its cool waters might have seemed close to desperately thirsty men, but actually lay twelve kilometres away. The Christian army now attempted to change direction and promptly fell into confusion. Saladin, who almost certainly had a clear view from hills to the south, realized what they were trying to do and sent Taqi al Din's division to block the way to Hattin. If Taqi al Din were still in command of Saladin's right wing his men would have been skirmishing with Count Raymond's troops since the Muslim main force committed itself to battle. Raymond, knowing that the Muslims would attempt to stop him seizing the spring at Hattin, urged speed but this proved impossible. Just how Taqi al Din got ahead and to the left of the Christians' vanguard is unclear. Perhaps his troops had been on the small hillock north-east of Lubia, blocking the main road to Tiberius. Being faster than their foes they could have moved sharply right, perhaps now anchoring their right flank on a larger hill by the village of Nimrin. This would have blocked the track from Manescalcia to the edge of the plateau and thence to Hattin spring. But this could have opened up the main road due east once again, so Saladin may also have moved the Muslim centre farther to the right. The Sultan certainly set up his headquarters on the hill of Lubia village the following night.

Gökböri, with Saladin's left wing, would have been on hills around Sejera and it was probably his troops whose determined attacks on the Latin rearguard forced King Guy to order another halt. The Templars charged in the hope of driving their tormentors away but failed. It was then that Count Raymond announced, 'Alas! Alas! Lord God, the war is over. We are betrayed to death and the land is lost.' He also advised Guy to have the exhausted army make camp around Manescalcia, though others urged an attack on Saladin's own position as the only remaining chance of victory. This time the King took Raymond's advice, perhaps hoping his army

would be able to strike out for Hattin spring in proper formation the following morning. Meanwhile Saladin's troops harassed them until nightfall.

The hills around the spot where the Christian army made camp were then quite wooded. Taqi al Din's division held the open plateau between Nimrin and the Horns of Hattin while Saladin's held the hills around Lubia. Nothing is known of Gökböri's division but this is likely to have closed the valley up which the Christians had just marched. During the night both sides are said to have been so close that their pickets could talk to one another. Thirsty and demoralized, the Latin army listened to the drums, prayers and singing of their enemies, while conditions in the Muslim camp were very different. That night Saladin brought up the rest of his troops from Cafarsset, presumably including the infantry. Four hundred loads of arrows were distributed, the troops having used up most of their immediate supplies. Seventy camels loaded with more bundles of arrows as a reserve were made ready to be sent where needed on the morrow. While the Christians gasped with thirst, the Muslim army had a caravan of camels carrying goat-skins of water up from Lake Tiberius. These were emptied into make-shift reservoirs dug in the camps of each Muslim division. Morale was, of course, high. Saladin's men also collected brushwood from the surrounding hills which would have been full of bone-dry thistles at that time of year. These they piled on the windward side of the Christian camp to be lit the following morning. It also seems that brushwood was placed along the Christians' expected line of march.

▶ *View from the northern Horn of Hattin looking south-west towards the modern kibbutz Lavi beyond which lay the abandoned village of Lubiyah. King Guy probably attempted to make a defensive camp here at the foot of the Horns. (Author's photograph)*

THE BATTLE OF HATTIN

Before dawn on the morning of 4 July 1187 the Christian army awoke and formed up ready to move. Count Raymond again commanded the vanguard, accompanied by Raymond of Antioch with his contingent. The Latin army was already in a bad way but Saladin did not disrupt its preparations, perhaps unsure whether it would make a dash for Hattin village or a desperate attack on his own position. Quite when the Muslims set fire to their stacks of brushwood is also unclear. Some say they did so before the enemy set off, others as they marched, or as the crumbling Christian force retreated to the Horns of Hattin. Given Saladin's careful preparations,

these fires may have been lit in sequence as the enemy marched. The final fires were ignited by volunteers; the shifting of the prepared stacks of kindling was a task suited to Saladin's numerous but untrained *muttawiya*. The Muslims also taunted the Christians by pouring water on the ground, this coming from the temporary cisterns dug the night before.

It may have been now that one or more knights with experience of serving in Islamic armies urged King Guy to make a sudden attack on Saladin's own position. But they were overruled and the army began its march to the Hattin spring which lay only five kilometres away.

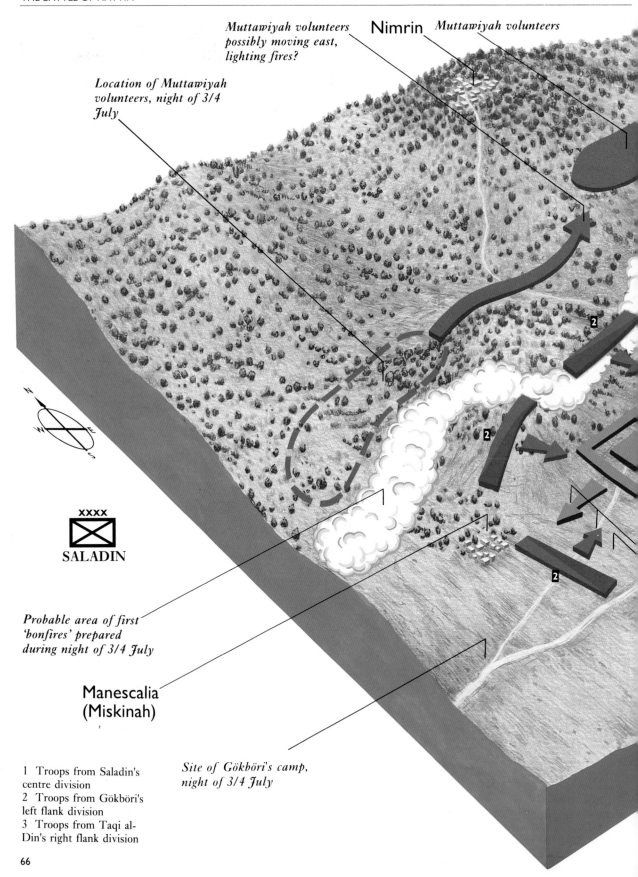

Muttawiyah volunteers
possibly moving east,
lighting fires?

Nimrin

Muttawiyah volunteers

Location of Muttawiyah
volunteers, night of 3/4
July

XXXX
SALADIN

Probable area of first
'bonfires' prepared
during night of 3/4 July

Manescalia
(Miskinah)

Site of Gökböri's camp,
night of 3/4 July

1 Troops from Saladin's
centre division
2 Troops from Gökböri's
left flank division
3 Troops from Taqi al-
Din's right flank division

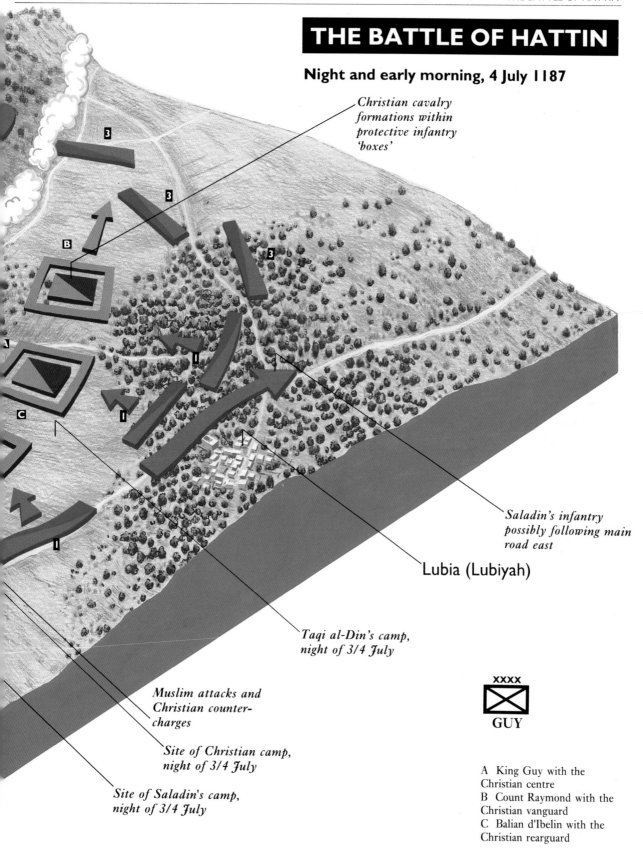

THE BATTLE OF HATTIN

Night and early morning, 4 July 1187

*Christian cavalry
formations within
protective infantry
'boxes'*

*Saladin's infantry
possibly following main
road east*

Lubia (Lubiyah)

*Taqi al-Din's camp,
night of 3/4 July*

*Muslim attacks and
Christian counter-
charges*

*Site of Christian camp,
night of 3/4 July*

*Site of Saladin's camp,
night of 3/4 July*

XXXX

GUY

A King Guy with the
Christian centre
B Count Raymond with the
Christian vanguard
C Balian d'Ibelin with the
Christian rearguard

So bad was the Christians' thirst and morale that six knights and some serjeants chose this moment to desert to Saladin, telling him that their comrades were as good as beaten. They included Baldwin de Fotina, Raulfus Bructus and Laudoicus de Tabaria. Saladin now seems to have sent his centre, and perhaps his left flank under Gökböri, into the attack. The Templars counter-charged while Count Raymond's vanguard also made a charge, presumably against Taqi al Din and the Muslim right wing who blocked the way forward. The only chronicler to hint at how near the Christians came to breaking through is Ibn Khallikan in his biographies of

Gökböri and Taqi al Din. 'They both', he wrote, 'held their ground although the whole army was routed and driven back. The soldiers then heard that these two chiefs still resisted the enemy, whereupon they returned to the charge and victory was decided in favour of the Muslims.' Saladin also lost one of his most trusted young

*amir*s named Manguras, early in the battle. He was probably fighting in the right wing, having previously served as Taqi al Din's deputy governor in Hama. Manguras charged forward alone and one source says that he challenged a Christian champion to fight him man-to-man but was thrown from his horse, dragged into the

◀ *Aerial view of the battlefield of Hattin seen in the late afternoon. The abandoned village of Nimrin lay in the rugged hills on the left, the abandoned village of Hattin at the foot of the shadowed gorge in the centre. The Horns of Hattin appear in the lower right corner and here the walls of an ancient, perhaps Bronze Age, settlement are clearly visible. (Israel Exploration Society)*

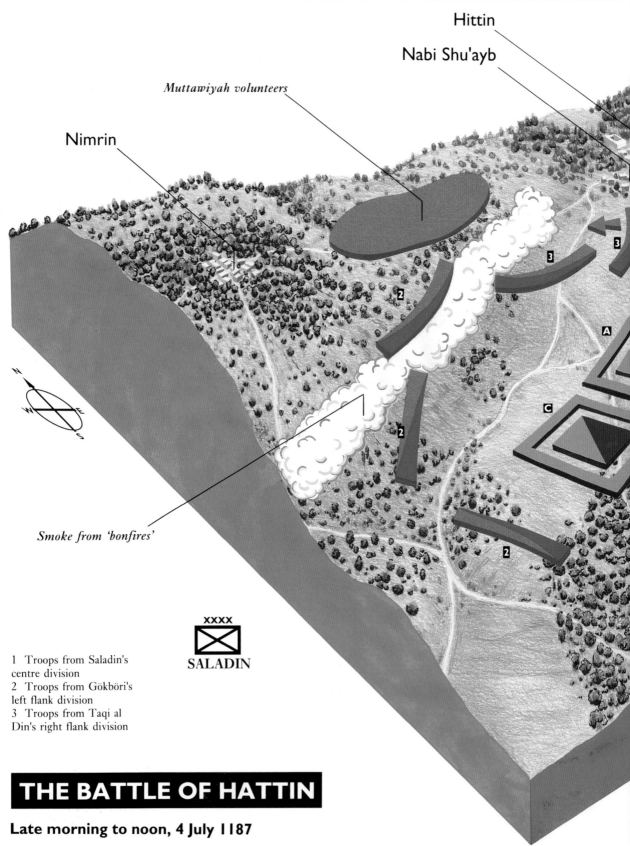

Hittin

Nabi Shu'ayb

Muttawiyah volunteers

Nimrin

Smoke from 'bonfires'

XXXX
SALADIN

1 Troops from Saladin's
centre division
2 Troops from Gökböri's
left flank division
3 Troops from Taqi al
Din's right flank division

THE BATTLE OF HATTIN

Late morning to noon, 4 July 1187

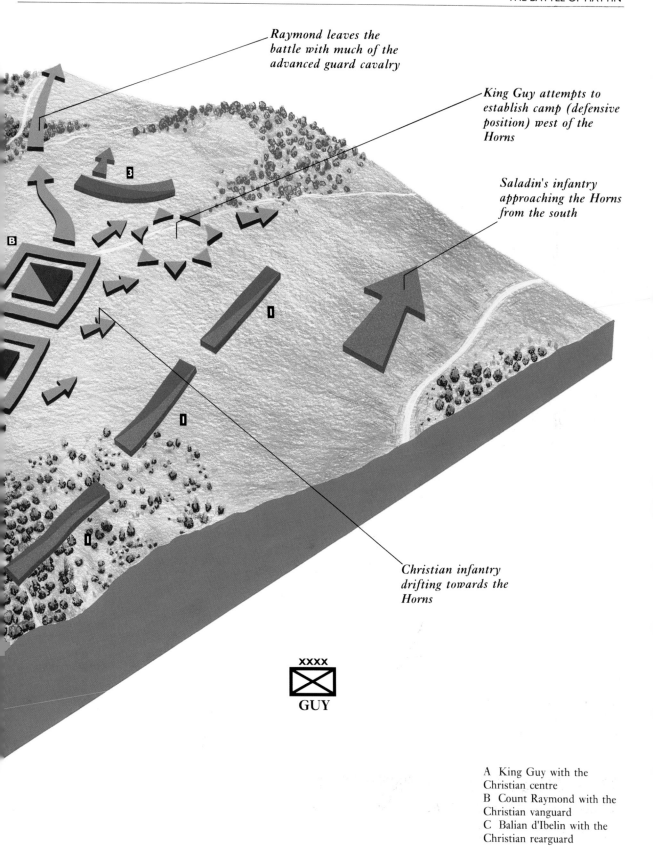

Raymond leaves the battle with much of the advanced guard cavalry

King Guy attempts to establish camp (defensive position) west of the Horns

Saladin's infantry approaching the Horns from the south

Christian infantry drifting towards the Horns

XXXX

GUY

A King Guy with the Christian centre
B Count Raymond with the Christian vanguard
C Balian d'Ibelin with the Christian rearguard

enemy lines and beheaded. Another states that he was simply overwhelmed by numbers.

The Christian army had set out in its standard formation with ranks of infantry, including archers and crossbowmen, protecting the cavalry while the latter stood ready to drive back the Muslims with controlled charges. The cavalry did drive back Saladin's first attacks but also lost many horses. More importantly, however, the morale of the Christian infantry now cracked and numbers started to drift eastwards. Muslim sources assume that the thirsty foot soldiers were heading towards Lake Tiberius, though this was much farther away than the spring at Hattin. Christian chroniclers state that the infantry sought refuge on the Horns of Hattin. What both original sources and most modern historians fail to explain is how they got through the middle of what should have been Saladin's army! Joshua Prawer, the greatest expert on the battle, assumed that Saladin had turned his entire army round the previous night, making Taqi al Din's division the left wing, Gökböri's the right, and placing his own central division somewhere to the west of the Latin forces. But Saladin's main position during the night had been at Lubia to the south, and his

◀ *View from the northern Horn of Hattin looking west. The closest hill may be where the Muslim dead of the battle were buried. Beyond it is the deep cleft down which Count Raymond and his men rode out of the battle after Taqi al Din's division swung aside to let them pass. Beyond that is another cleft and the wooded hills around the abandoned village of Nimrim. (Author's photograph)*

◀ *Looking down the gorge towards Hattin springs through which Count Raymond's cavalry escaped. The tomb of Nabi Shu'ayb (Jethro) is now a modern shrine sacred to the Arab Druze sect. (Author's photograph)*

primary objective was still to stop the enemy reaching water — either at Hattin village to the north-east or Lake Tiberius to the east.

A possible explanation is that Taqi al Din blocked the path to Hattin by holding a position from the foot of the Horns to Nimrin hill, that the centre of the Muslim army was arrayed between the foot of the Horns and Lubia hill blocking the main road to Tiberius, and that Gökböri's division stood between Lubia and the massif of Jabal Tur'an blocking any retreat west to the spring at Touraan village. Anchoring one's flanks on hills was a common tactic in Turco-Muslim cavalry armies, whereas placing a hill at the centre was more characteristic of infantry forces. Clearly Saladin feared that the Christians might break out towards Lake Tiberius and he gave strict orders that they be stopped. This suggests that Count Raymond's first charge had weakened the link between Taqi al Din's division and Saladin's. If this were the case, the Christian infantry who drifted eastward may have hoped to reach the lake which could still have been visible to the right of the Horns. If Saladin now extended the right of his own division he would have shepherded any enemy drifting east on to the Horns of Hattin. In an effort to provide a barrier against further attacks by Muslim cavalry, King Guy ordered his army to halt and put up tents, but in the confusion that followed only three were erected 'near a mountain' — almost certainly a short distance west or south-west of the Horns. Smoke from the burning brushwood certainly now played its part, stinging the eyes of the Christians and adding to their appalling thirst. The wind was, as usual at this time of year, from the west which suggests that the *muttawiya* were acting almost independently in the wooded hills between Jabal Tur'an and Nimrin. Any Muslim troops still around the Horns of Hattin would also have suffered from this smoke unless a clear gap had now opened between Saladin and Taqi al Din's positions.

At about this time Count Raymond of Tripoli made his notorious charge northwards and consequently escaped the débâcle. This was not, however, an act of treachery but an attempt to force a break in the Muslim ring and enable the army to reach water at Hattin village. The charge was probably ordered by King Guy. One thing is certain; instead of trying to stop Raymond, Taqi al Din had his more nimble soldiers swing aside and let the Christians continue down the gorge. Some writers, still imagining 12th-century European knights to be juggernauts weighed down by armour, assume that the momentum of Raymond's cavalry hurtled them down the path to Hattin village, but this is fanciful. Taqi al Din's men promptly returned to their positions at the top of the path, making it virtually impossible for Raymond to turn and charge back up the steep and narrow track. In fact Raymond had no alternative other than to continue across the fields beyond Hattin and down Wadi Hammam to Lake Tiberius. From there he chose not to join his wife in the trap of Tiberius but rode north to Tyre.

On the plateau confusion in the Christian ranks was getting worse and most of the infantry were now streaming towards the Horns of Hattin where they took up a position on the northern Horn. This might be significant, for if Taqi al Din had pulled his men up to Nimrin hill to let Raymond past he would have enlarged or finally opened up a gap between himself and Saladin's troops south of the Horns. Perhaps the Christian infantry had been moving north-eastward in support of Raymond's charge or had simply tried to follow Raymond in hope of escaping. Once the path to Hattin had been closed again it would be natural for them to drift left towards the smaller but closer northern Horn. Morale now collapsed with the infantry on this northern Horn refusing to come down and rejoin the cavalry who were still fighting around three tents at the foot of the Horns. King Guy ordered and the bishops begged. They must defend the Holy Cross, but the foot soldiers replied, 'We are not coming down because we are dying of thirst, and we will not fight.' Meanwhile the unprotected horses of the knights were struck down by enemy arrows until most knights were also fighting on foot.

There was now nothing for Guy to do but order his army on to the Horns of Hattin where the knights took position on the larger flat-topped southern Horn. The Royal tent, bright red and visible from a great distance, was probably set up

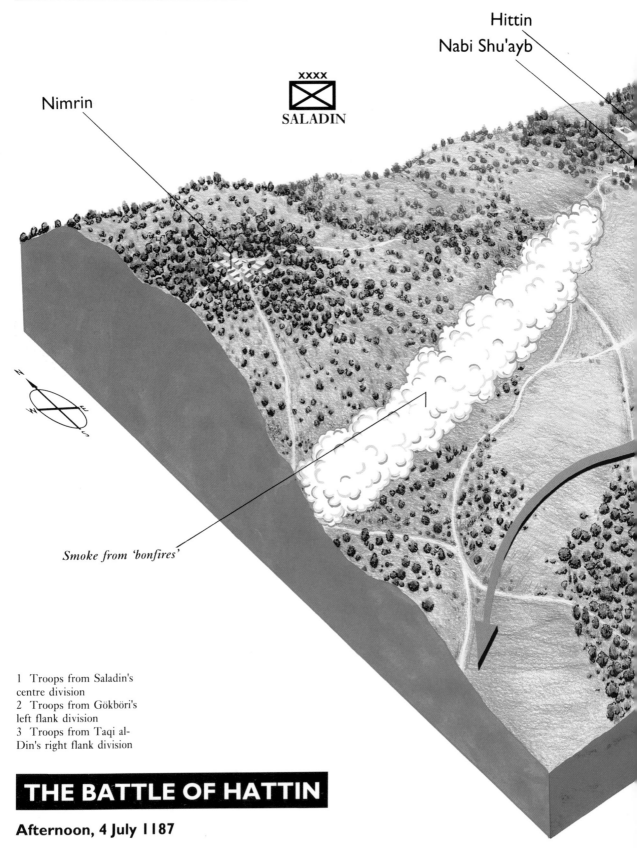

Hittin

Nabi Shu'ayb

XXXX

SALADIN

Nimrin

Smoke from 'bonfires'

1 Troops from Saladin's centre division
2 Troops from Gökböri's left flank division
3 Troops from Taqi al-Din's right flank division

THE BATTLE OF HATTIN

Afternoon, 4 July 1187

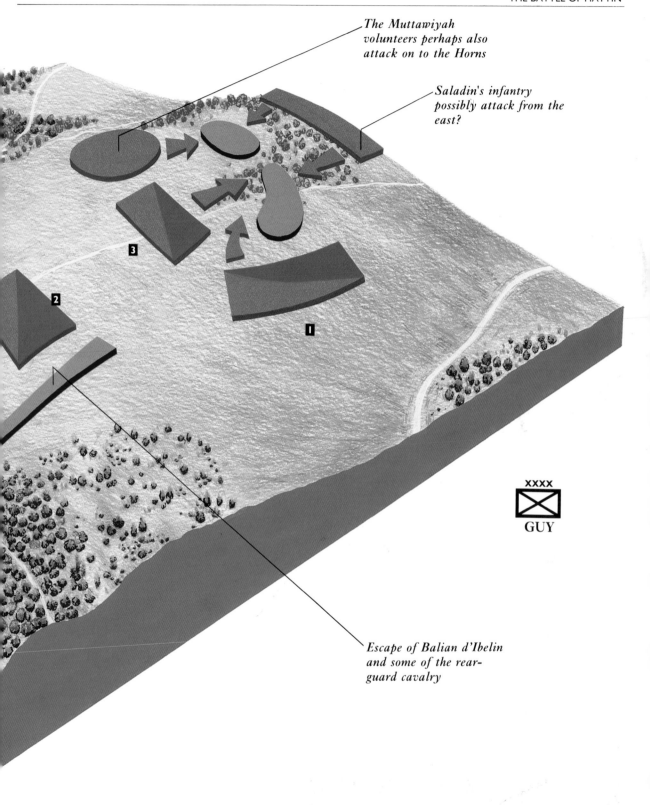

*The Muttawiyah
volunteers perhaps also
attack on to the Horns*

*Saladin's infantry
possibly attack from the
east?*

3

2

1

XXXX
GUY

*Escape of Balian d'Ibelin
and some of the rear-
guard cavalry*

on the southern Horn. Quite when the Holy Cross was captured remains unknown, though it was clearly seized by Taqi al Din's division. Some sources suggest that Taqi al Din made a fierce charge after allowing Count Raymond to escape and that the bishop of Acre, who carried the Cross, was killed, the holy relic then being taken by the bishop of Lidde before falling into Taqi al Din's hands. Others suggest that the bishop of Lidde took the Holy Cross up on to the southern Horn where it was finally captured during one of the last charges by Taqi al Din's troops. Whenever it happened the moral effect of the loss of this relic must have been devastating.

The Muslims now attacked the Horns of Hattin from all sides. The northern and eastern slopes are too precipitous for cavalry although a steep path does climb the northern side of the northern Horn. Muslim infantry now took on the Christian foot soldiers early in the afternoon and after a bitter struggle those Christians who were not killed or thrown down the slopes surrendered. Saladin also ordered Taqi al Din to charge the Latin knights as they made their last stand on the

▲ *View along a rubble 'rampart' on the western side of the saddle between the Horns of Hattin, looking north. The rubble in the foreground may also* have served the Christians as a barrier against Saladin's horsemen. *(Author's photograph)*

southern Horn. It would have been impracticable, though not impossible, for horsemen to attack up the southern slopes, and Saladin himself would have been covering this sector. So it seems likely that, while the Muslim infantry fought on the northern Horn, Taqi al Din rode up the gentle western slope that led between the Horns. For their part those Latin knights who still had horses regrouped, probably in this flat space, and made two vigorous counter-charges. One came close to Saladin himself who urged his men on, crying out, 'Away with the Devil's lie!' It may be that the Latins still hoped to slay the Sultan and snatch victory at the very moment of defeat. That they came close enough to endanger Saladin suggests that the centre of the Muslim army had now come right up to the south-western foot of

▲ *The southern Horn of Hattin seen from the northern Horn. Here the Latin cavalry, mostly dismounted having lost their horses to Saladin's archers, made a last stand. King Guy's tent could finally have been erected either on the northern Horn or in the flat saddle between the Horns. (Author's photograph)*

the Horns. Twice the Muslim cavalry charged up the slope, finally winning control of the saddle between the Horns. Young Al Afdal was at his father's side and cried out, 'We have conquered them!', but Saladin turned and said, 'Be quiet! We shall not have beaten them until that tent falls.' Even as he spoke the Muslim horsemen fought their way on to the southern Horn; someone cut the guy-ropes and the Royal tent fell.

That, as Saladin had predicted, marked the end of the battle. The exhausted Christians threw themselves to the ground and were captured without further struggle. Remarkably few of the well-armoured knights had been killed or even wounded, though the losses of horses and infantry was far higher. Nothing is recorded of Gökböri and the Muslim left wing during these last stages.

His division may have found itself almost out of the battle as the Latin army was swallowed up between Saladin and Taqi al Din. On the other hand a number of knights from the Latin rearguard, including its leader, Balian d'Ibelin, escaped near the end of the battle. Reginald of Sidon may also have got away at this time. Perhaps this indicates some carelessness on the part of the normally reliable Gökböri and maybe the Muslim chroniclers did not want to cast a shadow on a great victory.

Among those taken captive were King Guy, his brother Geoffrey de Lusignan, the *Connetable* Amalric de Lusignan, Marquis William de Montferrat, Reynald of Châtillon, Humphrey de Toron, the Master of the Templars, the Master of the Hospitallers, the bishop of Lidde and many other leading barons. Virtually the entire leadership of the Kingdom except for Count Raymond, Balian d'Ibelin and Joscelyn de Courtnay had fallen into Saladin's hands. Obviously feeling generous after his staggering victory, the Sultan offered a cup of cooled sweetened water to King Guy, but after he drank

Guy passed the cup to Reynald of Châtillon whom Saladin had sworn to kill. According to Arab custom a man who had taken food or drink from his captor was thereafter safe from harm. 'This criminal was given water without my consent,' observed the Sultan, 'and as such my safe-conduct does not extend to him.' Reynald knew that his doom was sealed and answered Saladin's question with arrogant courage until at last the Sultan's patience snapped. Whether he himself killed Reynald de Châtillon or ordered his men to strike off the Lord of Oultrejordain's head depends on which chronicler one believes. Saladin then placed a finger in his enemy's blood and rubbed it into his own face as a sign that he had taken vengeance. Not surprisingly the other captives were terrified but now the symbolic act was over the Sultan assured them that they were safe. Victors and vanquished remained on the battlefield that night but the following day, 5 July, Saladin rode down to Tiberius where Countess Eschiva surrendered her citadel.

All captured *Turcopoles* would, as renegades from the Muslim faith, probably have been killed on the battlefield. The rest of the prisoners reached Damascus on 6 July and there Saladin made a decision which has been seen as a blot on his humane record. All captured Templars and

◄ *The precipitous north-eastern slopes of the Horns viewed from the edge of the saddle between the two Horns. Even Saladin's light cavalry could not have operated effectively here and this was probably where his infantry made their assault. In the distance is the massive gorge of the Wadi Hammam leading down to Lake Tiberius. (Author's photograph)*

▶ *The summit of the Horns of Hattin looking from the southern Horns, where King Guy and his knights made their final stand, to the northern Horn where the Christian infantry fled earlier in the battle. (Author's photograph)*

▶ *A track winds around and up the southern Horn of Hattin to the saddle between the Horns. Here Taqi al Din's right flank division and Saladin's central division made several charges before the Latin army finally surrendered. (Author's photograph)*

Hospitallers were given the choice of converting to Islam or execution. Conversion under threat of death is contrary to Muslim law but on this occasion Saladin seems to have considered that the Military Orders, as dedicated fanatics with a bloody record of their own, were too dangerous to spare — 230 being slaughtered. A few converted and one Templar of Spanish origin later commanded the Damascus garrison in 1229, though if he were a survivor of Hattin he would have been a very old man. Other knights and leaders were ransomed but many of the infantry went into slavery.

Perhaps as many as 3,000 men from the Latin army escaped from the Battle of Hattin and fled to nearby castles and fortified towns. Some time later Saladin had a small monument, the *Qubbat al Nasr* or Dome of Victory, built on the Southern Horn. Nothing now remains, although its foundations were recently discovered. Muslim dead would have been buried with honour though it is not known where. A possible location could be the ruined Muslim shrine of Shaykh al Lika ('Old man of the Encounter') just to the north-west of the Horns overlooking the spring of Hattin.

THE CONQUEST OF THE KINGDOM

Events now unfolded at astonishing speed. On 7 July Saladin sent Taqi al Din to seize Acre which, contrary to expectations, resisted. Saladin himself arrived outside the walls on the 8th, but as the Muslims prepared their assault envoys came out to discuss terms. These were soon agreed, though there was rioting among the citizens when they heard the news. Saladin actually invited the Western merchants and feudal élite to remain under his rule but few if any of the inhabitants accepted. The fall of Acre also released the Byzantine Emperor's brother who had been held by the Latins. Saladin promptly sent him home and thus strengthened his already good relations with Byzantium. Meanwhile Al Adil was ordered

to invade southern Palestine with the Egyptian army which advanced rapidly and captured the powerful castle of Mirabel (Majdalyabah). The conquest of Acre also altered the naval situation by providing the Egyptian fleet with a base on the Palestinian coast for the first time since 1153, and a squadron of ten galleys was immediately sent from Alexandria. Saladin now split his forces into several sections, since there was no enemy field

▼ *The southernmost inner walls of Ascalon curving round to enclose the site of the medieval city, with the sea in the distance. The city would also have enclosed fields or gardens and, being on a flat sandy coastal plain, had doubled walls. (Author's photograph)*

army to fear, and sent them to mop up the various provinces of what had been the Latin Kingdom of Jerusalem. In many areas the local Muslim peasants and Jews rose in revolt, confining their Latin overlords and settlers in scattered castles until Saladin's troops arrived. The quantity of plunder and the number of prisoners taken was staggering, not to mention the 4,000 Muslim slaves who were released from Acre alone. By the end of the campaign more than 20,000 Muslims had been released while in return Saladin's men took more than 100,000 Latins captive.

Yet there were already problems. Taqi al Din had tried and failed to seize Tyre (Sur). Reginald of Sidon, having escaped from Hattin, got there first and took command as hordes of Latin refugees flocked in from all over the northern part of the Kingdom. He learned that his great castle of Belfort (Al Shaqif Arnun) still held out. Even so Reginald seems to have opened negotiations for a peaceful hand-over while Taqi al Din went inland to besiege the exceptionally strong castle of

Toron (Tibnin). Then Conrad of Montferrat supposedly took command of Tyre. The story of his arrival from Constantinople and seizure of command on 14 July has been seen as a turning-point, but it now seems that instead of sailing into Tyre in the midst of surrender negotiations Conrad really arrived one month later. Even if it were Reginald of Sidon who kept the Christian banners flying over Tyre in those desperate first months, Conrad's arrival clearly had a major impact on morale and the city went on to become the rallying point from which a truncated Latin Kingdom would later be reconquered.

Having left Acre on 17 July, Saladin led a lightning campaign up the coast of what is now Lebanon before returning to Tyre which was put under a loose blockade while Reginald retired to Belfort. From there he again negotiated with Saladin, offering Belfort in exchange for a position and pension in Damascus while in reality strengthening the castle's defences. Many of Saladin's troops now wanted to go home. The harvest was in and *iqta* holders needed to check

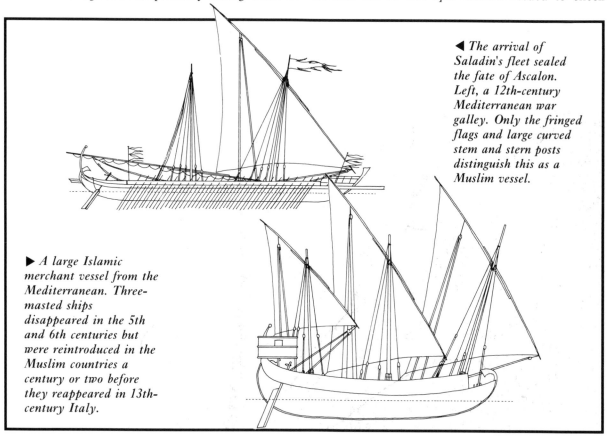

◀ *The arrival of Saladin's fleet sealed the fate of Ascalon. Left, a 12th-century Mediterranean war galley. Only the fringed flags and large curved stem and stern posts distinguish this as a Muslim vessel.*

▶ *A large Islamic merchant vessel from the Mediterranean. Three-masted ships disappeared in the 5th and 6th centuries but were reintroduced in the Muslim countries a century or two before they reappeared in 13th-century Italy.*

that their revenues had been collected. Neglecting their wives for more than four months could also give the women grounds for divorce under Muslim *ila* laws. Saladin clearly feared that his great army might drift away before he could take the greatest prize — Jerusalem. But before Saladin could attack Jerusalem he had to clear the enemy from the coastal ports through which help might flow from the west. Al Adil's Egyptian army was already operating in this area having taken Jaffa, Jerusalem's main outlet, in July. By the time the Sultan joined Al Adil on 23 August the Kingdom of Jerusalem had been reduced to Gaza and a few other isolated castles in the south, Ascalon, Tyre, Safad and perhaps still Belfort in the north, the castles of Oultrejordain almost forgotten in the east, and of course Jerusalem. But the key to southern Palestine remained Ascalon (Asqalan) until the arrival of the Egyptian fleet under Husam al Din Lu'lu to blockade the city sealed its fate.

The siege of Ascalon began on 25 August and by the following day the Muslims had taken the outworks. The siege was far from easy, however, and cost Saladin the lives of two of his best *amir*s including the chief of the Banu Mihran bedouin tribe. Negotiations eventually started and on 5 September Ascalon accepted the same generous terms as Acre, the garrison being allowed to leave with their families. They were then escorted to Egypt where they were given decent housing until repatriation to Europe. On that same day a delegation from Jerusalem arrived in the victor's camp — but they did not come with an offer of surrender. The remaining Latin castles and towns of southern Palestine then fell in quick succession before or during Saladin's final march on Jerusalem which he reached on 20 September.

Not surprisingly the morale of Saladin's army was high as it marched to Jerusalem. Discipline only wavered once when the fortified abbey of Bethany (Al Azariyah) was sacked, perhaps in reaction to a successful sortie by Jerusalem's garrison which killed an *amir* who, according to Ibn al Athir, had been advancing without proper caution. Despite the disasters suffered by the Kingdom of Jerusalem, the Christian garrison still had plenty of fight left and scoured the region for

supplies before Saladin arrived. The Patriarch Heraclius was in charge but he was no soldier. An eclipse of the sun had also increased the sense of impending doom. Then Balian d'Ibelin arrived. He had been in Tyre when Saladin gave him safe conduct to fetch his family from Jerusalem. On reaching the Holy City, however, Balian was surrounded by people urging him to take command of their defences. Heraclius even absolved him from his promise to Saladin. Torn between honour and his religious duty, Balian wrote a letter to the Sultan explaining that he had no choice but to take command and bid defiance to the man who had given him safe conduct. Saladin in turn seems to have accepted this from a man he regarded as a friend — though still an enemy. Balian d'Ibelin now reorganized the city's defences with typical efficiency and churches were stripped of their treasures to pay fighting men. Jerusalem was also full of refugees eager to fight. Nevertheless trained soldiers were few.

Having arrived before Jerusalem on 20 September, Saladin and his engineers studied the walls while the army made camp. At dawn the following day Saladin's troops attacked the north-western corner of the city between the Bab Yafa (David Gate) and the Bab Dimashq (St. Stephen Gate). Both sides yelled their battle cries and arrows poured down on the defenders. All surgeons in the city were employed plucking them from the bodies of the wounded. The anonymous author of *De Expugnationae Terrae Sanctae* records that he himself was struck on the bridge of his nose and that 'the metal tip has remained there to this day'. *Mangonels* of various kinds bombarded the walls, towers and gates while the Christians' own engines on the Towers of David and Tancred kept up a counter-barrage. The defenders fought with fanatical fury and made several effective sorties, damaging Saladin's siege engines and driving his troops back to their protected camps. Parts of the defences were damaged by powerful stone-throwing engines but not enough to force a breach. For five days both sides kept this up. The morning sun would be in the attackers' eyes, giving an advantage to the defence, while in the afternoon the opposite was the case. Muslim engineers even loaded their

The Siege of Jerusalem

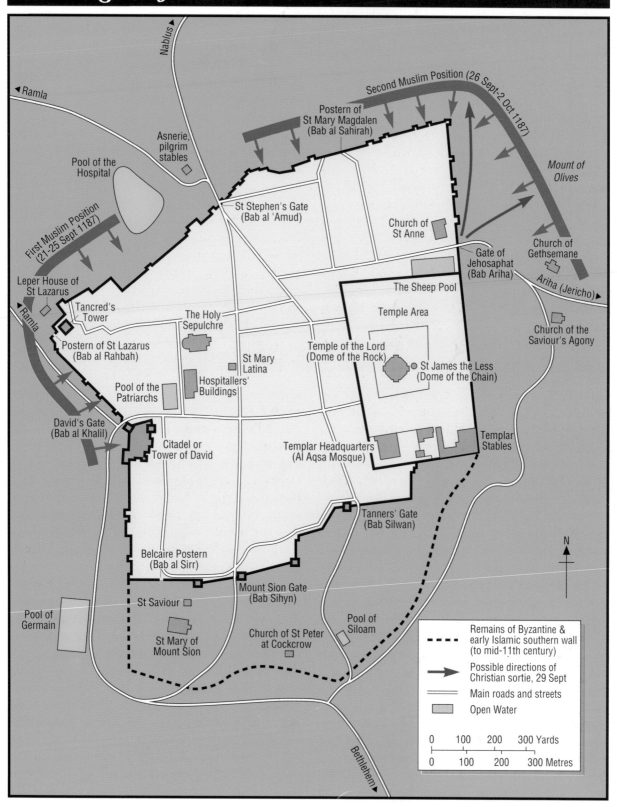

Nablus

◄ Ramla

Second Muslim Position (26 Sept–2 Oct 1187)

Postern of
St Mary Magdalen
(Bab al Sahirah)

Asnerie,
pilgrim
stables

Mount of
Olives

Pool of the
Hospital

St Stephen's Gate
(Bab al 'Amud)

Church of
St Anne

First Muslim Position
(21–25 Sept 1187)

Church of
Gethsemane

Gate of
Jehosaphat
(Bab Ariha)

Ariha (Jericho) ►

Leper House of
St Lazarus

The Sheep Pool

◄ Ramla

Tancred's
Tower

Temple Area

Church of the
Saviour's Agony

The Holy
Sepulchre

Postern of St Lazarus
(Bab al Rahbah)

St Mary
Latina

Temple of the Lord
(Dome of the Rock)

St James the Less
(Dome of the Chain)

Pool of the
Patriarchs

Hospitallers'
Buildings

David's Gate
(Bab al Khalil)

Citadel or
Tower of David

Templar Headquarters
(Al Aqsa Mosque)

Templar
Stables

Tanners' Gate
(Bab Silwan)

Belcaire Postern
(Bab al Sirr)

N

Pool of
Germain

Mount Sion Gate
(Bab Sihyn)

St Saviour

Pool of
Siloam

St Mary of
Mount Sion

Church of St Peter
at Cockcrow

Bethlehem ▼

Remains of Byzantine &
early Islamic southern wall
(to mid-11th century)

Possible directions of
Christian sortie, 29 Sept

Main roads and streets

Open Water

| 0 | 100 | 200 | 300 Yards |

| 0 | 100 | 200 | 300 Metres |

mangonels with sand which, driven by the prevailing wind, blew into the eyes of the defenders while assault parties tried to win the walls. Muslim losses were heavy and included senior men such as the *amir* Izz al Din Isa whose father held the beautiful castle of Jabar overlooking the Euphrates in northern Syria.

By 25 September Saladin realized that his men were making no headway against the western walls so the attack was called off. The *mangonels* were dismantled, the tents pulled down and the troops marched out of sight behind the hills. For a while the defenders thought that the siege was over, but the following day, 26 September, the Muslims reappeared to the north of Jerusalem. Even by the Christians' own admission this caught the defence off guard and the Muslims quickly erected *zaribas* cut from olive trees to protect themselves as they established a new siege position. From there they attacked the northern walls as well as the northern sector of the eastern wall. Their main effort was focused east of the Bab Dimashq, a notoriously weak sector of the defences, but a part of which had a doubled wall

which seems to have extended east beyond the small Bab Sahirah (Herod's Gate). There was also a small postern in the north-eastern stretch of the walls through which a sortie could be made, but it was difficult to use because of the doubled wall.

Up to forty *mangonels* were said to have been erected and these hurled rocks and *naft* (Greek fire). At least one was probably a new and powerful counterweight *trebuchet* and according to Balian d'Ibelin's squire, Ernoul, it struck the wall of the city three times on the very day that the Muslims renewed their siege. Next day Saladin sent forward three selected battalions of armoured engineers who advanced beneath large shields while archers gave covering fire. Having reached the ditch they began demolishing the base of the outer wall. Elaborate devices were erected, some covered with sturdy wooden roofs, beneath which Muslim miners cut away at the foundations. One tunnel, dug in two days, ran for 30 metres and was supported by wooden props which, when burned away, brought down a wide swathe of the wall on 29 September. To guard against sorties from the Bab Dimashq Saladin kept a large force

◀ *'David's Tower', the Citadel of Jerusalem, seen from within the city. The lower part is of Crusader work but the upper part probably dates from the Ottoman restoration of Jerusalem's defences in the 16th century. (Author's photograph)*

▶ *The Laqlaq Tower at the eastern end of the northern walls of Jerusalem. The First Crusade in 1099 and Saladin's army on 29 September 1187 both broke through the Holy City's defences a short distance to the right. (Author's photograph)*

of armoured cavalry on standby. The defenders also found the covering fire so intense that they were unable to shoot at the sappers while the rain of rocks from Saladin's siege machines hindered their countermining efforts. It is worth noting that the so-called Solomon's Quarry lies beneath the northern wall between Bab Dimashq and Bab Sahirah. If the Muslim miners could have reached these tunnels extending beneath the city they could have worked with virtual impunity.

A desperate sortie by every man in Jerusalem who had horse and weapons was made through the Bab Ariha (Jehosaphat Gate) but why they chose this gate is unclear for it led directly down a steep slope into the Kidron valley. Perhaps they hoped to cross the valley and attack Saladin's headquarters on the Mount of Olives opposite. Perhaps they tried to follow a narrow path beneath the city wall and come around the Laqlaq Tower to catch the Muslims in their flank. The attempt was, however, crushed by Saladin's cavalry.

With about 60,000 people inside the walls, refugees as well as the Latin, Syriac-Jacobite and Orthodox Christian inhabitants, opinions varied on what should now be done. The Patriarch Heraclius and other barons promised to pay 5,000 'bezants' — an enormous sum — and distribute weapons to any fifty serjeants who would guard the newly made breach for a single night. They were not found for it was clear that Saladin's final assault was due. On the other hand other leading citizens proposed a suicidal night sortie, seeking death in battle rather than slaughter within the walls. Heraclius, however, dissuaded them by pointing out that they might win Paradise but they would leave women and children to lose their souls by abandoning Christianity.

On 30 September Balian d'Ibelin, as a personal friend of the Sultan, was sent to the Muslim camp where Saladin was already in contact with the non-Latin Christian communities within Jerusalem. Relations between the Latins and the Syriac-Jacobites had always been bad but now relations with the Orthodox were also at a low ebb. Joseph Batit, one of Saladin's closest aides and an Orthodox Christian born in Jerusalem, was actually negotiating with his co-religionists to open a gate in the north-eastern quarter of Jerusalem where most of them lived. Balian's negotiations were hard but not long. Twice he was refused an audience while an attempt by Saladin's troops to seize the breach was driven back. Next day Balian returned to Saladin's camp to learn that the Sultan had been discussing the matter with his *amirs* and religious advisers. Should the Holy City be taken by storm and the defenders slaughtered as they had slaughtered the Muslim and Jewish inhabitants in 1099? Saladin reminded Balian how the offer of honourable surrender made to Jerusalem's delegation outside Ascalon had been scornfully rejected. He also pointed out that he had sworn to take Jerusalem by storm and was known as a man of his word.

Perhaps believing that any sign of weakness would make matters worse, Balian threatened that if necessary the garrison would kill its own families, its own animals, the 5,000 Muslim prisoners still in its hands, destroy its own treasures, demolish the Dome of the Rock and the Aqsa Mosque — among the holiest buildings in Islam — then march out to meet Saladin's troops, '...thus we shall die gloriously or conquer like gentlemen'. Whether this threat showed that the fanaticism of the First Crusaders was still alive in Jerusalem, or whether it was a last desperate gamble, no one knows. But neither Saladin nor his officers seem prepared to risk a holocaust worse than that of 1099. Instead a peaceful surrender was agreed for 2 October, on which day Saladin's banners were raised over Jerusalem and trusted *amirs* posted at each gate.

The non-Latin Christians could remain but the invading Crusaders must go. Every man was to pay 10 dinars, with 5 for every woman, 1 for each child. A lump sum of 30,000 bezants would pay for 7,000 poor people who could not afford their own ransoms. Saladin allowed forty days for the money to be paid. Now it was time for haggling over ransoms, though most of the quarrelling was within the Christian ranks. The Military Orders seemed unhappy about using their accumulated treasure to help those poor who could not pay ransoms and there is doubt about how hard Heraclius tried to help those unable to pay. The Latins could take any property they could move, but much was sold in the *suq al askar* which always followed Saladin's army. When the forty days was up there were still many poor trapped without means of paying for their freedom. So while the Christian rich struggled down the road to the coast laden with what valuables they could carry, Saladin himself paid the ransoms of many poor people. So disgusted were Saladin's *amirs* at the lack of Christian charity that they urged their Sultan to confiscate the wealth flowing out of the Bab Yafa (Jaffa Gate). Saladin refused to break his agreement, but even so there were up to 15,000 still in Jerusalem when the deadline came.

Some of the leading ladies of the Kingdom were also found in the city. King Guy's wife Sibylla was taken to see her husband now imprisoned in the citadel of Neapolis (Nablus) and the Lady Stephanie, widow of Reynald de Châtillon, was given her son, captured at Hattin, in return for ordering the garrisons of Krak and Montreal to surrender. When they refused, the Lady sent her son back to Saladin who was so struck by this honourable gesture that he soon let the young man go again. Even before the last ransoms were paid, the Muslims re-entered the Holy City to reclaim it for Islam. Their first task was to cleanse various buildings, making them fit for worship once more. On 9 October 1187 Saladin and many senior religious figures entered Jerusalem to make their *salat* (prayers) in the restored Al Aqsa Mosque. New buildings were commissioned while a palace once used by Patriarch Heraclius was given to *sufis* (Muslim mystics) as a convent. The headquarters of the Hospitallers became a religious college while most of the Latin churches were handed over to other Christian sects.

The fall of Jerusalem did not mean the end of the struggle. An unrecorded campaign was still being fought east of the Jordan where the remaining Latin possessions around the Yarmuk valley fell. Far to the south in Oultrejordain the castles of Montreal and Krak did not fall until 1188 and 1189 respectively. Meanwhile the defenders of Tyre recovered their confidence and sat tight behind the walls of a city built on a rocky peninsula that could only be approached across a narrow, sandy isthmus. They were also supported by numerous ships. Saladin was determined to renew the siege of Tyre and returned to the area with a small force on 12 November, the rest of his army coming up to assault the city thirteen days later. It was a hard fight, the attackers being supported by as many siege engines as could be trained on the enemy. The isthmus was narrow and Christian ships filled with archers, crossbowmen and stone-throwing engines were moored on each side to shoot at the Muslims' flanks. The attacks failed and the siege dragged on with occasional attacks by the Muslims and frequent sorties by the defenders, among whom a Spanish knight, dressed in green and with a pair of stag's horns in his helmet, earned praise even from Saladin himself.

It was now clear that only by winning command of the sea could Tyre be taken, so a squadron of ten galleys and an unknown number of support vessels came up from Acre under the command of Abd al Salam al Maghribi, an experienced North African sailor. This was highly risky in the squalls of winter — the Mediterranean sailing season normally running from early April to late October — but the Muslim fleet did force the Christian galleys into harbour. Meanwhile winter arrived, the besiegers' camp becoming a sea of mud and slushy snow as sickness broke out.

Then came disaster at sea. A Muslim squadron of five galleys, having kept watch through the night of 29/30 December, lowered their guard with the coming of dawn, but as they slept they were surprised by a fleet of seventeen Christian galleys with ten smaller boats which darted out of Tyre and captured them. The five remaining Muslim galleys and other ships were then ordered to retire to Beirut because they were now too few to be effective. As they left they were pursued by galleys from Tyre which soon overhauled the exhausted Muslim crews. Most were beached, their crews escaping ashore and the vessels being destroyed on Saladin's orders, though one large sailing ship, described as being 'like a small mountain' and manned by experienced sailors, was able to escape. Following

this setback the troops made a final unsuccessful attack on the defences of Tyre after which Saladin summoned a conference of his *amirs*. Some wanted to fight on but most said that the army was exhausted and their men wanted to go home, so next day, New Year's Day 1188, Saladin dismissed his army except for his own personal regiments whom he led back to Acre.

▼ *Unlike Asqalan and some other coastal cities, Jerusalem was crammed with narrow streets and houses. In September 1187 it would also have been full of refugees. Once the city had surrendered to Saladin on 2 October, the Muslims returned to reclaim the sacred* *buildings occupied by Latin Christians for almost a century. The most important would have been the Aqsa Mosque hidden to the right of this picture and the Dome of the Rock, here seen down Bab al Qattan-ayn Street. (Author's photograph)*

AFTERMATH AND RECKONING

The events of 1187 shook western Europe, the loss of Jerusalem being seen as casting shame on all Christians. On 20 October Pope Urban III died, of grief it was said. Nine days later his successor, Pope Gregory VIII, sent out letters urging Christendom to save what was left of the Crusader Kingdom, letters which eventually led to the Third Crusade. On 19 December Pope Gregory also died. Meanwhile the survival of Tyre was a military disaster for Saladin, providing a perfect base from which the Third Crusade would start reconquering a rump Kingdom of Jerusalem in 1191. Yet this revived Crusader Kingdom was never what it had been. Hattin had demolished its feudal structure and undermined the basis of royal power. Western European interference in its government also increased rapidly.

On the Muslim side the liberation of Jerusalem had an enormous impact on Saladin's prestige. Barely noticed amid the excitement, a merchant caravan had set out from Damascus on 23 September, even before Jerusalem fell, heading for Cairo by the coastal route. It was the first for more than eighty-seven years to travel this route without paying tolls.

Performance of the Muslim Army

The Battle of Hattin was a typical encounter of its kind in which Saladin relied on varied but long-established tactics. Muslim morale may have been superior as a result of the Latin leaders' decision to lead their men on an exhausting, thirsty march, but although the Christians blundered, Saladin showed obvious tactical superiority. In the end the battle was won by the superior military capabilities of the Muslim troops in the situation in which the two armies fought. With better logistical support, superior speed of manoeuvre, greater ability to change position while retaining cohesion and probably better battlefield communications, one might think that the Muslims were bound to win — but in many other clashes they had not. Muslim capabilities in close combat have often been denigrated on the grounds that they wore lighter armour, wielded lighter weapons and rode smaller horses. The former two points are over-simplifications while the third is probably just wrong. In the end Hattin was won because Saladin got his enemies to fight where he wanted, when he wanted and how he wanted.

Performance of the Christian Army

Christian morale and potential may have been damaged by a previous defeat at the Springs of Cresson, while the events surrounding that smaller battle had clearly undermined the prestige of the Latin army's ablest commander, Count Raymond of Tripoli. Sir Charles Oman's suggestion that the Latin army could have reached water at the Wadi al Hammam, many kilometres north of Hattin, was almost certainly wrong. In fact the only major mistake that King Guy made was marching east from Sephorie in the first place. Having made that decision, however, he and his advisers seem to have done whatever they could, and probably whatever they should, to trap Saladin in a disadvantageous position. Once battle was joined, the Christian army stuck to the tactics which had served it well in the past. The fact that these now failed was partly because of improvements in the opposing Muslim forces, but mostly because of the exhaustion of the infantry. They in turn let their cavalry down by failing in their primary task of protecting the knights' horses. Horse-armour may have been used in the Latin army but would have been extremely rare in

 بذ كردون وهامون خروش مصیبت شذان شادی ونازونوش
شبیغم كردن نبیع ابن عذناح

شذ بس راز مرد تمشنه زن كدبك بش شمت ریشاء شبر

▲ 'Night attack by Rabi ibn Adnan', from the late 12th- to early 13th-century Warqa wa Gulshah manuscript from Azarbayjan. Two horsemen wearing large helmets and lamellar jawshans plus mail hauberks beneath their tunics, are armed with long single-edged swords and large round shields. They are supported by two unarmoured foot soldiers. (Topkapi Library, Istanbul, Ms. Haz. 841)

▶ 'Chedorlaomer captures Lot', on the mid 13th-century painted ceiling of the Parma Baptistry in Italy. Here the mailed horsemen on the right wear relatively light armour of a kind suited to the hot climates of Italy or the Latin States, but which would by now have been regarded as old-fashioned in France or England. Chedorlaomer is portrayed in archaic and unrealistic Roman armour.

1187. It would also have made the knights even more unwieldy than they were. The supposed military-technological superiority of the European armoured knight is still accepted by many historians who should know better. Given the circumstances in which he had to fight in the Middle East, we should leave the last word with Saladin's friend and biographer, Baha al Din:

'A Latin knight, as long as his horse was in good condition, could not be knocked down. Covered by a mail hauberk from head to foot... the most violent blows had no effect on him. But once his horse was killed, the knight was thrown and taken prisoner.'

THE BATTLEFIELDS TODAY

Saladin's campaign of 1187 ranged over five countries — Syria, Lebanon, Jordan, Israel and Egypt, the Israeli-occupied sections of what may yet become a fifth country — Palestine — plus the Israeli-occupied portions of Syria and Lebanon. Nevertheless, most of the sites involved are quite easy to visit and the Horns of Hattin themselves lie next to an hospitable *kibbutz* which includes a first-rate hotel.

Tal 'Ashtarah and Tasil where Saladin's army mustered lie south of the little town of Nawa in the fertile Province of Dara'a south of Damascus. Unfortunately this is only 10 kilometres from the Syrian-Israeli cease-fire line, within a UN-policed area which even Syrian citizens need permits to enter. These can be obtained in Damascus but can take several days. Busra, like all other regions, towns and castles in Syria, welcomes visitors. No part of Jordan is subject to permits though before trying to visit the spectacular cave-fortress at Ayn Habis it is advisable to check with the authorities as the caves actually overlook a sensitive frontier.

Four-wheeled drive vehicles are not necessary in Syria or Jordan though a car with good ground clearance is advisable when using unmade roads. Taxis are cheap and abundant throughout this part of the world whereas hire-cars are expensive. Local bus services are cheaper still but only link the main villages. Good hotels are found in Damascus, Dara'a, Irbid, Amman, Karak and Petra, adequate *funduq*s (small hotels for local travellers) being found in all small towns. Most of the Lebanese castles and cities involved in Saladin's campaign lie in the turbulent south of the country, some actually within the Israeli-occupied frontier strip, and at the time of writing travel in this area could be considered hazardous. Otherwise the same type of transport and accommodation are available as in Syria and Jordan. The same applies in Egypt except that a four-wheeled drive vehicle is strongly advised when one leaves the surfaced roads in Sinai.

The main sites of the 1187 campaign lie in Israel, occupied East Jerusalem, the West Bank and Gaza Strip. In Israel proper travel can, to the surprise of many western visitors, be more difficult than in the neighbouring Arab countries. Most holiday-makers stick to the beaches or carefully sanitized visits to major archaeological sites. But those who go off the beaten track find settlements and small towns where strangers, other than those visiting relatives, are rare. While the main tourist centres have excellent hotels, the countryside lacks small hostelries comparable to the *funduq*s of neighbouring Arab countries. There are, however, camp-sites and *kibbutzim* which offer excellent though sometimes expensive accommodation. Political temperatures are high in the occupied territories at the time of writing (January 1992) but otherwise the same information concerning types of vehicle, public transport and accommodation apply as in Syria or Jordan. Saladin's army only transited the Golan Heights, though it camped for one night outside the now dynamited village of Khisfin. Unlike the other tense occupied territories, the Golan is quiet for the simple reason that the inhabitants were expelled at gunpoint in 1967.

The battlefield of Hattin lies at the eastern edge of *kibbutz* Lavi and is easily approached by a track which turns north off the main Haifa-Tiberius road (Route 77) just east of the Horns of Hattin. Almost all the villages that featured in the campaign were destroyed by the Israelis following the 1948 War and their inhabitants expelled. The people of Tur'an survived, however, as did those of Ayn Mahil overlooking what were the Springs of Cresson. Saffuriyah Castle is still there but nothing remains of the village except for fragments of houses amid

▶ *The marshy area known as Al Qahwani (Cavan) to the south of Lake Tiberius, seen from Khirbat Aqaba on the Israeli-occupied Golan Heights. The town of Tiberius is some distance to the right on the far side of the Lake. The old road which Saladin's army followed goes straight ahead to the flat lands where they camped on 27 June before crossing the Jordan. (Author's photograph)*

▶ *All that now remains of the village of Hattin, destroyed by the Israelis in 1948, is a minaret among the tangled bushes around Hattin spring. The Arab village itself is largely buried beneath the expanding Tiberius city rubbish tip from which this picture was taken. (Author's photograph)*

the tress. Lubiyah now consists of scattered rubble overgrown with thistles and surrounded by the trees of a memorial park while Nimrin has also been obliterated. The tomb of Nabi Shu'ayb, however, has become a flourishing shrine for the Druze sect. In front of it stands a car-park laid over a rubbish tip which is itself gradually swallowing up the abandoned remains of Hittin village. To the south Kafr Sabt, where Saladin established his headquarters, has again been replaced by an Israeli settlement. Tiberus of course remains, though its main mosque now appears to be a storeroom for a neighbouring cafe. The so-called Crusader Citadel north of the old town is an 18th-century structure, but recent excavations to the south have uncovered what are believed to be a Crusader church and part of the walls of the original Arab-Crusader town.

91

CHRONOLOGY

1187:

Winter Reynald of Châtillon captures Muslim caravan.

13 March Saladin sets up camp at Ras al Mai' and summons troops to *jihad*.

20 March Al Adil leads Egyptian forces towards Aqabah. The Hajib Lu'lu' takes warships to Alexandria.

29 March Taqi al Din reaches Aleppo to guard the northern frontiers.

Early April Saladin leads contingent south of Busra to protect pilgrims.

26 April Saladin attacks Krak.

29 April Delegation leaves Jerusalem to seek reconciliation with Count Raymond.

30 April Envoy from Al Afdal asks Count Raymond's permission for reconnaissance party to cross the Count's lands.

1 May Muslim reconnaissance force attacked by Christian forces near Springs of Cresson, defeats the Christians and returns same day.

27 May Saladin instructs Ayyubid forces to muster at Tal 'Ashtarah. King Guy instructs his army to gather at Sephorie.

26 June After reviewing his army Saladin marches off, making camp at Khisfin. King Guy holds a Council of barons at Acre.

27 June Saladin's army camps at Al Qahwani, reconnaissance parties sent into Christian territory.

28-9 June Christian army completes muster outside Sephorie.

30 June Saladin makes camp near Cafarsset (Some scholars believe that Saladin did not cross the Jordan until 2 July).

1 July Saladin approaches Christian army at Sephorie then makes reconnaissance of Lubia area.

2 July Part of Muslim army attacks Tiberius which falls except for Citadel.

Night of 2/3 July King Guy decides to relieve Tiberius.

3 July Christian army marches towards Tiberius. Saladin leaves a small force to watch Tiberius. Christian army forced to stop at Manescalcia.

Night of 3/4 July Saladin organizes troops and supplies.

4 July Christian army defeated at HORNS OF HATTIN.

5 July Countess Eschiva surrenders Tiberius Citadel.

8 July Muslim army arrive outside Acre.

10 July Acre surrenders to Saladin.

14 July Tyre breaks off surrender negotiations with Saladin.

26 July Toron surrenders to Saladin.

29 July Sidon surrenders to Saladin.

4 August Gibelet surrenders to Saladin.

6 August Beirut surrenders to Saladin.

25 August Saladin and Al Adil start siege of Ascalon.

5 September Ascalon surrenders to Saladin.

20 September Muslim army reaches Jerusalem.

25 September Muslim army stops attacking western wall of Jerusalem.

26 September Muslim army starts attacking northern wall of Jerusalem.

29 September Breach made in wall.

2 October Jerusalem surrenders to Saladin.

1 November Saladin sends army to besiege Tyre.

30 December Combined land and naval attack on Tyre beaten off.

1 January 1188 Saladin disbands half his army, raises siege of Tyre.

A GUIDE TO FURTHER READING

Most primary sources have been published, the main Islamic ones having been translated into a European language and are listed in the bibliographies of all serious studies of the Crusades. General accounts of 1187 are found in all histories of the Crusades, but several more detailed descriptions are listed here:

BALDWIN, M. *Raymond III of Tripolis and the Fall of Jerusalem*. Princeton, 1936. Focuses on the roll of Raymond.

BLYTH, E. 'The Battle of Hattin', in *Palestine Exploration Fund Quarterly Statement*, LIV, 1922.

DALMAN, G. 'Schlact von Hattin', in *Palästina-Jahrbuch*, 1914.

EHRENKREUTZ, E.S. 'The Place of Saladin in the Naval History of the Mediterranean Sea in the Middle Ages', in *Journal of the American Oriental Society*, LXXV, 1955.

— *Saladin*. New York, 1972. A more critical biography than earlier accounts.

ELBEHEIRY, S. *Les Institutions de l'Egypte au temps des Ayyubides*, Service de Reproduction des Thèses, Université de Lille, III, 1972.

FULLER, J.F.C. *The Decisive Battles of the Western World*. London, 1954. Outdated and simplistic but still useful.

GIBB, H.A.R. 'The Armies of Saladin', in *Cahiers d'Histoire Egyptienne*, III, 1951.

HAMILTON, B. 'The Elephant of Christ: Reynald of Châtillon', in *Religious Motivation: Biographical and Sociological Problems for the Church Historian: Studies in Church History*, XV, ed. D. Blake, Oxford, 1978.

KEDAR, B.Z.(ed.). *The Horns of Hattin: Proceedings of the Second Conference of the Society for the Study of the Crusades and the Latin East*, Jerusalem and London, 1992.

LANE-POOLE, S. *Saladin and the Fall of Jerusalem*. London, 1898. A traditional account, idealizing the main protagonist.

LYONS, M.C., and JACKSON, D.E.P. *Saladin, the Politics of the Holy War*. Cambridge, 1982. The best account based on a proper understanding of the Islamic context.

NICHOLSON, R.L. *Joscelyn III and the Fall of the Crusader States, 1134-99*. Leiden, 1973.

PRAWER, J. 'The Battle of Hattin', in *Crusader Institutions*, Oxford, 1980; previously published as 'La Bataille de Hattin' in *Israel Exploration Journal*, XIV, 1964. The best analysis of the battle based on knowledge of the ground. The only weakness is in minor aspects of Islamic military equipment and tactics. It also contains a full bibliography, including small articles on specific aspects of the political circumstances, campaign and battle.

REGAN, G. *Saladin and the Fall of Jerusalem*. London, 1987. A general account which makes use of recent research.

SMAIL, R.C. 'The Predicaments of Guy of Lusignan, 1183-87', in *Outremer*, ed. B.Z. Prawer, Jerusalem, 1982.

INDEX

(References to illustrations are shown in **bold**.)